BRING FORTH *your* RECORD

A Guide to Preserving Spiritual Experiences

Praise for

Bring Forth Your Record: A Guide to Preserving Spiritual Experiences

---

This book will make you smile. Rachel writes in such an authentic and accessible way that you can't help but want to record your own stories.

Steven Sharp Nelson, The Piano Guys

Read, use, and remember these helpful motivations and fantastic examples to preserve your own spiritual experiences. Your life is worth preservation and Matthews teaches how to start.

Annalisa Hall, best-selling author of
The Holy Ghost is Like a Blanket

Rachel helps us see or recognize what Heavenly Father teaches us, usually in small and simple ways. Much of what God reveals sails over our heads unnoticed because we are not looking. *Bring Forth Your Record* helps us to see more clearly the hand of God pouring down knowledge from heaven on our heads, especially in the day-to-day details of life. Rachel's greatest contribution is to help us remember by making a record of what we learn.

Elder Lawrence E. Corbridge,
emeritus General Authority Seventy

Rachel shares compelling reasons to write about the promptings and answers we receive—then explains how to do it before we get distracted or discouraged! Bring Forth Your Record will expand your definition of 'personal revelation' and help you notice more miracles in your own life.

John Bytheway, best-selling author
and cohost of the followHim podcast

A warmly personal and deeply faithful book. This sparkling combination of witty and moving stories, useful patterns, and practical steps will help individuals of all ages create valuable personal records.

Neill Marriott, former counselor
in the Young Women General Presidency

BRING FORTH *your* RECORD

A Guide to Preserving Spiritual Experiences

RACHEL MATTHEWS

CFI
An imprint of Cedar Fort, Inc.
Springville, Utah

Paperback ISBN 13: 978-1-4621-4583-6
Ebook ISBN:978-1-46214663-5

Published by CFI an imprint of Cedar Fort, Inc.
2373 W. 700 S., Suite 100, Springville, UT 84663
Distributed by Cedar Fort, Inc., www.cedarfort.com

Library of Congress Registration Number: 2023942311

Cover design by Shawnda Craig

Printed in the United States of America
10 9 8 7 6 5 4 3 2 1
Printed on acid-free paper

CONTENTS

CHAPTER 1

Becoming a Record Keeper

Therefore give heed to my words;
write the things which I have told you.[1]
Write the things which ye have seen and heard.[2]

—Jesus Christ

One day, after we read from the Book of Mormon, my youngest daughter, Scout, announced, "There's a book of Nephi, a book of Alma, a book of Moroni. . . . There should be a book of Scout!" In that moment, I felt like the Holy Ghost said to me, "There *could* be!" My initial excitement about the possibility grew into a desire to compile The Book of ______ for each of my kids. But because I didn't act on the idea right away, it slowly sank lower and lower on my mental list of good intentions until I forgot about my plan. It didn't get as low as "Make a baby blanket for Scout," who is now ten years old, but it slipped from my conscious thought.

Thankfully, I heard a unique analogy that brought it back up to the surface of my mind. During a general conference address, Elder Neil L. Andersen compared spiritual experiences to rocks:

> When personal difficulty, doubt, or discouragement darken our path, or when world conditions beyond our control lead

1. 3 Nephi 23:4.
2. 3 Nephi 27:23.

> us to wonder about the future, the **spiritually defining memories from our book of life are like luminous stones** that help brighten the road ahead, assuring us that God knows us, loves us, and has sent His Son, Jesus Christ, to help us return home. And when someone sets their defining memories aside and is lost or confused, we turn them toward the Savior as we share our faith and memories with them, helping them rediscover those precious spiritual moments they once treasured.
>
> Embrace your sacred memories. Believe them. **Write them down.** Share them with your family. Trust that they come to you from your Heavenly Father and His Beloved Son. Let them bring patience to your doubts and understanding to your difficulties. I promise you that as you willingly acknowledge and carefully treasure the spiritually defining events in your life, more and more will come to you.[3]

Elder Andersen's talk resonated with me because I have never outgrown my childhood love of rocks. Although I never mention it when another adult asks what I do for fun, I feel genuinely happy when I look for rocks up in the mountains, out in the desert, or at the ocean. Years before I heard the word "mindfulness," hunting for rocks and admiring them kept me completely present in beautiful places.

When our family hikes together, I see at least one rock that I can't stand to leave behind on the trail. By the time I pick up one that catches my eye, my kids usually have several in their pockets. For years, I enforced a rule that everyone had to carry their own rocks because I didn't want my backpack to get heavier and heavier throughout the hike. When my children were little and needed to keep their hands free for balance and climbing, I told them they could only bring home rocks that fit in their pockets.

One afternoon in Neffs Canyon, I found a large chunk of gray rock with a rust-colored inclusion in the center. Considering the cantaloupe-sized stone a unique piece of natural art, I carried the odd

3. Neil A. Andersen, "Spiritually Defining Memories" *Ensign*, May 2020; emphasis added.

shape in both hands and wondered who would point out my obvious disregard for our family guidelines. As I slowly crossed a small stream with this find, my son, Bear, teased, "What happened to, 'if it fits in your pocket, you can bring it home?'" And with that, I abolished every rule we had about rocks.

After transporting our treasures in pockets, backpacks, and bare hands, we display our new rocks on various surfaces around the house. Sometimes, we stack them into little cairns or arrange them in shallow bowls. However, several months later, those stones get relegated to the bottom of a catchall drawer and are eventually stored in shoeboxes and repurposed peanut butter jars under our beds. Every now and then (I won't admit how infrequently we deep clean), someone rediscovers one of these collections, dumps it out, and looks at the rocks one by one. Although a few stones remind us of specific places we explored together, more often we don't remember where most of them originated and someone will wonder out loud, "Why did I keep *this* one?" Once treasured, without their contextual meaning, most of them become just rocks.

Each of us have experienced moments when we received thoughts or feelings from our Heavenly Parents through the Holy Ghost. When I heard Elder Andersen's talk, the Holy Ghost reminded me about the Book of Scout and gave me another chance to gather my children's spiritually defining memories. This time, I decided to act, collecting journal entries, Primary and sacrament meeting talks, and notes from their priesthood blessings into inexpensive three-ring binders.

Then, I interviewed them about times when they had felt the Holy Ghost and typed simple paragraphs to journal those moments. My kids had seen me document other people's personal experiences before, so this didn't seem strange to them. For years, whenever a friend or family member shared a testimony-building story with me, I immediately asked, "Did you write it down?" Tortured by the possibility that the story would be forgotten or lose its significance, I would wait a few days, then call or text with a cheerful reminder. If they hadn't yet recorded the experience, I stopped nagging and offered to type everything I could remember and email it to them so they could use it as a starting point.

Are you a record keeper? Are your luminous stones easily accessible so they can renew your faith and the testimonies of others? If they currently lie under the bed in a dusty shoebox of forgotten memories, this book is *your* starting point, a way to collect your stories into a record that will have power in your life and in the lives of others. The books of Enos, Mosiah, and Helaman contain accounts of how God interacted with ordinary people in their imperfect lives. As you write the experiences when you felt loved, seen, and guided by God, you will become a record keeper who stands as a witness and creates a source of ongoing spiritual strength.

Writing about our faith-building experiences brings a multitude of blessings and benefits, including:

- As you record the moments when you felt the Spirit, you send a sign to God that you value those experiences.
- When you write down your memories, you get to relive those moments and enjoy them again.
- In addition to the good feelings that come from revisiting them, "remembering spiritual experiences . . . reinforces your faith."[4] Just like bearing your testimony aloud makes it stronger, writing your testimony reaffirms and solidifies your beliefs.
- Reading about your spiritual experiences may help your kids, grandkids, friends, and others, so taking the time to preserve your faith-building memories is one more way for you to help gather Israel.
- Your inspirational stories will be ready for you to easily incorporate into a future talk or lesson at church.
- When you encounter trials in the future, your written experiences can bring you comfort and motivate you to stay close to the Lord. You might even listen to your own advice when you aren't open to the counsel of others!
- Peace of mind and other blessings come from following the counsel of current and past prophets, who have asked us to record sacred experiences. Elder Joseph B. Wirthlin

---

4. Steven E. Snow, "The Sacred Duty of Record Keeping" *Ensign*, May 2019.

taught, "Obedience brings great strength and power into your lives."[5]

- Writing about Jesus Christ is a form a worship as we acknowledge and praise Him.
- Recording personal revelation increases our capacity to receive it!

Many prophets and apostles have taught that writing is part of learning to communicate with God. When President Russell M. Nelson instructed us to "stretch beyond your current spiritual ability to receive personal revelation," he also explained *how* to do it. Did you notice that in addition to "increased purity, exact obedience, earnest seeking, daily feasting on the words of Christ in the Book of Mormon, and regular time committed to temple and family history work," he also counseled us to write? He said: "Pray in the name of Jesus Christ about your concerns, your fears, your weaknesses—yes, the very longings of your heart. And then listen! **Write the thoughts that come to your mind. Record your feelings** and follow through with actions that you are prompted to take. As you repeat this process day after day, month after month, year after year, you will "grow into the principle of revelation."[6]

In general conference three years later, President Nelson again referred to writing in conjunction with increasing our spirituality. He asked, "What would you do if you had *more* faith?" Then he instructed, "Think about it. Write about it."[7]

If you want to enjoy the myriad of promised blessings that come from writing about sacred experiences but you feel stress, anxiety, or trepidation when you look at an empty page or blank screen, please know that these negative reactions are common. The daunting task of filling unstructured space with words makes many people freeze or walk away. Even those who desire to follow the counsel of Church

---

5. Joseph B. Wirthlin "Live in Obedience" *Ensign,* May 1994.
6. Russell M. Nelson, "Revelation for the Church, Revelation for Our Lives" *Ensign,* May 2018; emphasis added.
7. Russell M. Nelson, "Christ Is Risen; Faith in Him Will Move Mountains" *Liahona,* May 2021.

leaders to record sacred moments often express valid concerns that fall into three main categories:

- "I don't know where to start!"
- "I'm not a good writer!"
- "I can't think of any spiritual experiences!"

Temporary Obstacle #1: "I don't know where to start!"

As with most tasks and projects, figuring out where to start can feel like the hardest part. But the beauty of the story you are going to write is that you will begin in the middle! It's actually better to not worry about an introduction because nothing kills momentum like too much context. When I reread old journal entries, I find myself slogging through paragraphs and paragraphs of backstory before I reach the beautiful moment of connection that I originally intended to record. I regret that before I explained the exciting event, I always felt the need to explain the evolution of the relationships and feelings that led up to that moment. Besides messing up the backstory-to-actual-story ratio, that approach has even altered the tone of my entry, especially when a story about forgiveness no longer has a tone of relief and joy because I spent five paragraphs chronicling the months that I held a grudge.

So, please don't stress about an introduction. You will write that at the end, and by then you will find it surprisingly simple. We don't need to know who went on the hike, who forgot the sunscreen, or which songs you listened to on the car ride to the trailhead. Your story starts with the moment that you bent down and picked up a beautiful stone. The moment that the Holy Ghost answered your prayer. The moment that you felt unexpected and inexplicable peace. You can add backstory later. When you write your story out of order, some of the pressure of getting it "right" dissipates.

Temporary Obstacle #2: "I'm not a good writer!"

For many people, how to start is only one of the obstacles that inhibits momentum. The other stems from years in school when teachers handed back our papers covered with corrections in red ink. Trained to watch for errors, our brains tend to think about writing the way we think about math. When we solve math problems, our goal is to discover the single right answer. By contrast, when we created art in school, our teachers accepted many results as valid and valuable. You might have liked your tissue paper owl more than the owl glued together by the little boy across the table, or vice versa. But all the owls had a certain charm, and we celebrated the differences; we didn't point them out with a frown. In math, we compare our answers with others to see if we achieved the goal. But in art, every finished piece must be original; otherwise, we hold a copy, not a creation.

Writing falls somewhere between math and art, but most of us scoot it too far down the scale toward structured equations. Lurking in the back of our minds, Spelling and Grammar watch us for any misstep, ready to dock points and reduce our grade. But remember, no one will correct your story and give you a score. Anyone who reads it will feel grateful, not critical. We can trust that as members of our family hear our stories, they "will receive them with thankful hearts, and look upon them that they may learn with joy and not with sorrow, neither contempt."[8]

Think of every piece of your story as a little art project, a natural expression of an idea that doesn't have a "correct" or "incorrect" value. And if it helps you to think of it as a first draft, simply remind yourself that once you get the basic story written down, it's manageable and straightforward to polish it later—if you want to. (See chapter 8 for more on improving existing stories.) As you record your spiritual experiences, just write them the way you would tell these stories to a close friend. Don't try to sound smarter than you are. You are the perfect balance of smart, funny, serious, honest, and spiritual to tell your own story, The Book of __________. Go ahead and write your name on that line right now! You are now a record keeper.

As you flip through the starter questions at the end of every chapter, notice which one jumps out at you and sparks a memory. Whichever question resonates with you is the exact spot to start. And

---

8. Jacob 4:3.

as you consider the prompts, don't worry if you don't have answers to all of them. Even writing a paragraph in response to two or three will yield a beautiful and valuable record.

Temporary Obstacle #3: "I can't think of any spiritual experiences!"

Surprising things happen when we make our prayers as specific as possible. Ask our Father in Heaven to help you remember your spiritual experiences, and the Holy Ghost will bring thoughts to your mind. Elder Richard G. Scott taught, "Inspiration carefully recorded shows God that His communications are sacred to us. Recording will also enhance our ability to recall revelation."[9] And our Savior gave us this simultaneously reassuring and exciting promise:

> But the Comforter, which is the Holy Ghost, whom the Father will send in my name, he shall teach you all things, and **bring all things to your remembrance**, whatsoever I have said unto you.[10]

President Henry B. Eyring shared a personal experience that illustrates this principle:

> I came home late from a Church assignment. It was after dark. My father-in-law, who lived near us, surprised me as I walked toward the front door of my house. He was carrying a load of pipes over his shoulder, walking very fast and dressed in his work clothes. I knew that he had been building a system to pump water from a stream below us up to our property.
>
> He smiled, spoke softly, and then rushed past me into the darkness to go on with his work. I took a few steps toward

---

9. Richard G. Scott, "How to Obtain Revelation and Inspiration for Your Personal Life" *Ensign*, May 2012.
10. John 14:26.

> the house, thinking of what he was doing for us, and just as I got to the door, I heard in my mind—not in my own voice—these words: "I'm not giving you these experiences for yourself. Write them down."
>
> I went inside. I didn't go to bed. Although I was tired, I took out some paper and began to write. As I did, I understood the message I had heard in my mind. I was supposed to record for my children to read, someday in the future, how I had seen the hand of God blessing our family.
>
> I wrote down a few lines every day for years. I never missed a day no matter how tired I was or how early I would have to start the next day. As I would cast my mind over the day, I would see evidence of what God had done for one of us that I had not recognized in the busy moments of the day. As that happened, and it happened often, I realized that trying to remember had allowed God to show me what He had done. And I grew more confident that the Holy Ghost can bring all things to our remembrance—even things we did not notice or pay attention to when they happened.[11]

I love how the message President Eyring received didn't come after a magnificent miracle. The Holy Ghost instructed him to write about something seemingly ordinary. In the moment when he stood still and saw his father-in-law's gift of time with spiritual eyes, he recognized it as a blessing. Remember, "all things which are good cometh of God; wherefore, every thing which inviteth and enticeth to do good . . . is inspired of God."[12]

Elder Ronald A. Rasband explained the true criteria for a sacred experience this way: "Miracles, signs, and wonders abound among followers of Jesus Christ today, in your lives and in mine. Many of you have witnessed miracles, more than you realize. They may seem

---

11. Henry B. Eyring, "O Remember, Remember" *Ensign*, November 2007.
12. Moroni 7:13.

small . . . but the magnitude does not distinguish a miracle, only that it came from God."[13]

When we decide to define our spiritual experiences by the source, not the size, we will start to notice more miracles. And if you are not sure whether certain moments in your life deserve the label "personal revelation," writing about those experiences will invite the Holy Ghost to testify to your heart and mind, enabling you to make connections that you didn't see before.

We often call the small miracles in our lives "acts of service." President Kimball taught, "The Lord does notice us, and he watches over us. But it is usually through another person that he meets our needs."[14] When has someone met your needs? Maybe they deliberately fulfilled an errand from the Lord that day. Maybe they didn't even realize that they delivered a blessing. My mom used to tell us that we should always smile at an elderly person in the grocery store and say hello to them because "you will never know—you might be the only person who smiles at them in their whole day." Adamant that we learn this important lesson, she repeated the counsel more than any other specific admonition, and to this day, I cannot pass a white-haired customer in a grocery store without feeling a responsibility to show kindness.

We have the power to meet each other's needs in simple ways, and God has the power to meet our needs in more ways than we can imagine. Most of us have had a moment that we could call a coincidence or a tender mercy, depending on our perspective. When I discussed this concept with my friend Andy, even though he describes himself as "not religious," he immediately thought of an event in his life that he described as, "beyond good luck." Can you think of a moment like that? If so, you can summarize it in a sentence or two right here:

---

13. Ronald A. Rasband, "Behold! I Am a God of Miracles," *Liahona*, May 2021.
14. Spencer W. Kimball, "President Kimball Speaks Out on Service to Others" *Ensign,* March 1981.

____

____

____

____

____

____

____

____

You just started your story! Well done.

Elder Richard G. Scott encouraged, "You will find that as you write down precious impressions, often more will come."[15] Slowly, other memories will float up from your subconscious and surprise you because as your brain works on this project, you will receive spiritual help. When we work to build something that God wants us to create, He will help us "find ore to molten,"[16] or access source material for our heaven-endorsed project. President Camille N. Johnson, who served as both Primary General President and Relief Society General President, taught that the Savior, "the author and finisher of our faith,"[17] can also be "the author and finisher of your story."[18] If we allow Jesus Christ to guide our lives, He will also guide us as we bring forth the record of our lives. We simply need to take the first step by indicating our willingness.

When my dad taught my youth Sunday School class during my senior year of high school, he liked to balance his open scriptures on

15. Richard G. Scott, "To Acquire Knowledge and the Strength to Use It Wisely" *Ensign,* June 2002.
16. 1 Nephi 17:9.
17. Hebrews 12:2.
18. Camille N. Johnson, "Invite Christ to Author Your Story" *Liahona,* November 2021.

one hand and read from them as he taught. His flat palm and long, outstretched fingers made the perfect platform. With his other hand, he gestured to emphasize his sincere, articulate testimony. I only remember one lesson when he deviated from his typical style. Since I learn best from visual aids, his most memorable lesson for me occurred when he uncharacteristically held his copy of the Book of Mormon in both hands and opened and closed it several times in a row to teach us about willingness. He told us that the moment we open the scriptures—pausing to slowly open the Book of Mormon in front of us—we show God that we *want* to receive personal revelation. Because I previously associated receiving personal revelation with extraordinary need or tremendous effort, my understanding expanded as he taught us that before we even read a single word, God will bless us for that tiny act of obedience. Closing the scriptures again, he emphasized, "As soon as you *open* them, the scriptures become a conduit for the Holy Ghost to speak to you." I stared at the book, once again open in his hands, marveling at the abundant goodness of a God that will bless us for every small step toward Him.

With confidence, I testify that we can apply the same promise to writing our own sacred stories. Because the "Lord seeth not as man seeth," He doesn't look at the "outward appearance" of a person, an experience, or an empty page. Instead, He "looketh on the heart"[19] and sees the potential of an individual and the miracle in the seemingly ordinary moment. When we intend to record our spiritually defining memories, we qualify for heavenly help the moment we pick up a pen.

When Jesus Christ visited the Nephites, He didn't just ask whether they *remembered* the miracles they had witnessed; He also asked whether they had *recorded* the miracles:

> Behold, other scriptures I would that ye should write, that ye have not. And it came to pass that he said unto Nephi: **Bring forth the record which ye have kept**.

---

19. 1 Samuel 16:7.

> And when Nephi had brought forth the records, and laid them before him, he cast his eyes upon them and said: Verily, I say unto you, I commanded my servant Samuel, the Lamanite, that he should testify unto this people that at the day that the Father should glorify his name in me that there were many saints who should arise from the dead, and should appear unto many and should minister unto them. And he said unto them: Was it not so?
>
> And his disciples answered him and said: Yea, Lord, Samuel did prophesy according to thy words and they were all fulfilled.
>
> And Jesus said unto them: How be it that ye have not written this thing, that many saints did arise and appear unto many and did minister unto them? And it came to pass that Nephi remembered that this thing had not been written. And it came to pass that **Jesus commanded that it should be written**; therefore it was written according as he commanded.[20]

Starting today, you can keep this commandment to write about those who have ministered to you and the miracles you have seen. You can bring forth your record of how the Savior has influenced your life. As you compile your stories like the record keepers who contributed to The Book of Mormon: Another Testament of Jesus Christ, you will create The Book of _________: A Personal Testament of Jesus Christ.

20. 3 Nephi 23:6–7, 11–13; emphasis added.

CHAPTER 2

Recognizing the Holy Ghost

Our ability to hear spiritually is linked to our willingness to work at it. . . . [A] combination of faith and hard work is the consummate curriculum for learning the language of the Spirit.[21]

—Sheri Dew

Whether you learned to call the third member of the Godhead *the Spirit, the Holy Ghost,* or *the Holy Spirit,* hopefully you have experienced a moment when He delivered a message to you from God. Some people associate revelation with a warm sensation or a peaceful feeling, while others receive words or ideas in their minds. Elder David A. Bednar taught:

> A light turned on in a dark room is like receiving a message from God quickly, completely, and all at once. Many of us have experienced this pattern of revelation as we have been given answers to sincere prayers or been provided with needed direction or protection, according to God's will and timing. Descriptions of such immediate and intense manifestations are found in the scriptures, recounted in Church history, and evidenced in our own lives. Indeed, these mighty miracles do

21. Sheri Dew "We Are Not Alone" *Ensign*, October 1998.

> occur. However, this pattern of revelation tends to be more rare than common.
>
> The gradual increase of light radiating from the rising sun is like receiving a message from God "line upon line, precept upon precept" (2 Nephi 28:30). Most frequently, revelation comes in small increments over time and is granted according to our desire, worthiness, and preparation. Such communications from Heavenly Father gradually and gently "distil upon [our souls] as the dews from heaven" (D&C 121:45). This pattern of revelation tends to be more common than rare.[22]

This analogy helps me remember that not every piece of revelation impacts us in a grand or emotional way. If you can't think of an exact moment when you received personal revelation, you might be mentally scanning for something big and shiny through a telescope, instead of noticing miraculous detail through a microscope. Carol B. Thomas, first counselor in the Young Women General Presidency, said, "Spirituality is learning how to listen to the Spirit and then letting it govern our lives. . . . The Spirit doesn't always give us warm, fuzzy feelings. Most of the time, the voice of inspiration is a quiet voice, a still, small voice."[23]

To better identify how the Spirit communicates with you, consider some wonderful counsel from David Butler's incredible book, *Spirit: The Gift that Connects You to Heaven*. He first references how, for Elijah, "the Lord was not in the wind: and after the wind an earthquake; but the Lord was not in the earthquake: And after the earthquake a fire; but the Lord was not in the fire: and after the fire a still small voice."[24] Butler then contrasted that vehicle for revelation with the experience Moses had on that same mountain, where for him, the Lord was in the fire—a burning bush. We can learn a great deal from how "Elijah got a whisper, and Moses got a flame." Butler

---

22. David A. Bednar, "The Spirit of Revelation" *Ensign*, May 2011.
23. Carol B. Thomas, "Developing Our Talent for Spirituality," *Ensign*, May 2001.
24. 1 Kings 19:11–12.

goes on to say: "One of the best pieces of advice someone ever gave me when learning to recognize the Spirit was to ask God for help. Ask Him to help you learn the way He speaks to you. It will be a process, but remember that is exactly how He wants it. If it takes longer that means a longer amount of time you spend together—and that is exactly what He would hope for."[25]

Starters

- When did you most recently feel the Spirit?
- Does the Holy Ghost primarily communicate with you through thoughts or feelings?
- Has the Spirit ever delivered a message to you in another way?

Stories

You have probably attended a church lesson when the teacher asks for volunteers to share a personal experience. Maybe you started thinking about how you could answer. For many of us, by the time we come up with a relevant answer that we feel comfortable sharing, the discussion has progressed to another topic and sometimes even a new question. When I teach, I like to ask a question, then tell a story while people consider how they might answer. Many teachers effectively employ this technique by providing one possible answer to their own question to kick off brainstorming and give the class time to think of other answers. In a similar way, while you think about the questions in each chapter, I will share several stories that might remind you of spiritual moments in your own life.

* * *

For an entire year, the bishopric of our ward assigned every speaker in sacrament meeting the same topic. All of them focused

---

25. David Butler, *Spirit: The Gift that Connects You to Heaven* (Salt Lake City: Deseret Book, 2020).

their talks on answering the question, "How do you hear Him?" The resulting stories and testimonies revealed an enormous range of ways that Jesus Christ communicates with us, including uplifting music, the kind acts of others, strong feelings, nature, art, subtle impressions, and scriptures. When I experience personal revelation, I often receive clear ideas or sentences in my mind, but I have many family members who do not get words from the Holy Ghost. Instead, they associate certain feelings with the Spirit. To my surprise, I once had a sacred experience marked by the noticeable *absence* of a certain negative feeling! Countless disciples have used analogies about warmth to describe the Holy Ghost, but my son, Bear, says that when he feels the Spirit, "it's like jumping into a lake and finding out that the water is colder than you expected!" The methods that God uses to connect with His children seem as numerous and varied as His earthly creations. The *Preach My Gospel* manual instructs: "The Spirit is always available to guide and direct you. However, the Spirit speaks quietly, through your feelings as well as your mind. One great challenge for you . . . is to recognize the quiet, subtle promptings of the Holy Ghost."[26]

Sometimes, the Holy Ghost might barely brush our consciousness with simple suggestions. In other sacred moments, He might take our breath away with miracles. Hyperbole does not often go hand-in-hand with truth. My Grandma Joan used to say that my generation had stripped the word "awesome" of its original meaning by overusing and misapplying it. But even with these caveats in mind, I can authentically describe the following experience by telling you that it occurred on the loneliest and saddest night of my life.

My former husband and I implemented a 50/50 parenting time schedule with our kids when we announced our plans to get divorced. Following a color-coded calendar that I taped to the fridge, our kids slept at my house for two or three nights in a row, then slept at their dad's house for two or three nights. The exception to our schedule was our one-year-old, who slept in a crib at my house every night, even on the evenings when she had dinner at her dad's. We had agreed to give her the extra stability of a single place to sleep until she turned

---

26. *Preach My Gospel: A Guide to Missionary Service* (Salt Lake City: The Church of Jesus Christ of Latter-day Saints, version 3/19).

two years old, since we weren't sure if she could understand the new arrangement yet.

Snuggling her sturdy, pajama-clad body proved an effective antidote to heartache as I ended every day with a familiar and sweet routine. It eased my guilt to give her an extra ten months of normalcy. I also knew that I benefited immensely from her company and a sense of purpose each night. Knowing that she needed me helped me stay strong.

The week of Scout's birthday, when her dad took her to sleep at his house for the first time, I wondered how well I would deal with finally sleeping in my house alone. I decided to wrap up in a blanket and read the scriptures in an old banana chair (a floor rocker without legs) in our basement family room. But with an empty house and a grieving heart, I couldn't focus enough to find comfort in the beautiful words before me. The reality of shared custody crashed into me like an ocean wave made up of hundreds of images—all the nights when I couldn't tuck them in and all the mornings when I wouldn't see their bedhead hair and hear their sing-songy "good moooorning!" I thought about all the Friday nights when we wouldn't get cozy on the couch and watch a movie together, the holidays they wouldn't celebrate with me, the camping trips when they would do shadow puppets in the tent with a flashlight and I would not be there to guess the animals. I began to sob uncontrollably.

After a few minutes, the unfamiliar sound of my own hysterical voice started to scare me. I couldn't pull it together, couldn't take a deep breath like I had practiced hundreds of times in my hypnosis-for-childbirth classes. I rocked forward and fell onto the carpet on my knees, praying out loud in a desperate, repetitive cry, "Heavenly Father, please help me . . . please help me . . . please help me . . . please help me!" I couldn't form any better sentences but finally gasped out, "In the name of Jesus Christ, amen!"

The exact moment that I uttered the name "Jesus Christ," I stopped crying. My basement, suddenly silent, filled with a powerful sense of peace. I knew without a single doubt that I did not possess the ability to calm my emotions that quickly. The usual deceleration of heartbeat and breath somehow occurred instantly. I kept my eyes closed, using every ounce of my awareness to notice the peace in the air, as tangible as a change in humidity. I felt that I wasn't alone, and I kept my eyes closed so that my natural sight couldn't argue with what my spirit sensed. I sat silently for a few moments, and then the spiritual energy dissipated. I took a deep breath and opened my eyes, full of awe and gratitude.

Before leaving the basement, I prayed again—quietly this time—to thank God for rebuking the wind and waves in my heart.[27] I did not cry again that night but slept soundly. The next night, I did not cry. And the next night, my kids returned.

* * *

Like me, my mom describes her most memorable spiritual experience as a feeling of profound peace, even though she connected with God in entirely different circumstances. When my brother served a mission in Ukraine, he wrote a weekly email to our parents and siblings, who lived in three different states at the time. Each member of our family copied the rest of the group when we replied to our first and only family missionary, so the weekly correspondence became our virtual Sunday dinner together.

After a few weeks, our emails must have reminded him too much of listening to his three older sisters gossiping at the kitchen counter because he wrote home and asked if we could please share our recent spiritual experiences. We collectively cringed as we realized that we didn't have much to say. Looking back, I wonder if the Holy Ghost directed him to challenge us to look for the small miracles in our lives. Once we put forth a tiny bit of effort to notice and record them, we recognized the hand of God in our lives every week. So, years before group chats and messaging apps, our emails provided a forum for spiritual discussions that we had never attempted in person.

Without this weekly family email, I never would have heard about how my mom felt the Spirit deep in the ocean. She told us:

---

27. Mark 4:37–39.

> I think the most spiritual experience I have had was when I was scuba diving. I was amazed. It looked like someone had dumped a box of crayons into the ocean—one of the big, giant boxes! The colors were so beautiful, and the sea life was unbelievable. We saw a million fish like on *National Geographic,* and they all changed direction at the same time. We saw lobster that were bigger than a basketball.
>
> It was a drift dive along a reef, so no one had to swim or kick, we just floated along. It was so quiet and peaceful down there. Just then, out of the rocks, came the most magnificent manta ray that you could ever imagine. It was huge. It silently glided through the water toward us. I watched it for a long time. As its fins slowly moved up and down through the water, it looked so graceful. I was just in awe.
>
> When we got back up to the surface, I found out that our friend Mike had seen it, too, and we both felt close to tears because of the incredible sight.

My mom saw something truly "awesome," with the original, Grandma-approved definition. Witnessing one of God's unique creations in a completely quiet environment allowed my mom to feel connected to Him. Truly, "all things denote there is a God; yea, even the earth, and all things that are upon the face of it . . . do witness that there is a Supreme Creator."[28] Years later, she still treasures it as one of the great sacred events of her life. Aileen H. Clyde, who served as the second counselor in the Relief Society General Presidency, eloquently described this type of spiritual experience by saying: "Each of us has had the experience of matching a truth or a realization through inspiring words or music from others to something deep within our souls. When that connection happens, it feels like a small explosion of knowing. We are lifted and warmed; both our minds and our hearts are involved. These experiences, at least momentarily, verify our kinship with one another and with God."[29]

---

28. Alma 30:44.
29. Aileen H. Clyde, "Charity and Learning," *Ensign*, November 1994.

* * *

In bright contrast to her underwater moment of profound peace, my mom's most unusual spiritual experience didn't feel calm or quiet at all. It began when she fell off her horse and broke her arm above the elbow. Doctors used a metal plate and thirteen screws to set the bone, then directed her to wear a sling as she waited for her humerus to heal. Any jokes we made about the name of that bone failed miserably, since her arm didn't feel any better after six weeks. To her great disappointment, the X-ray at her follow-up appointment showed that absolutely no healing had taken place. The doctor explained, "When you break a bone, it usually excretes a sandy material that glues the bone back together. But the surgeon who set your arm must have cleaned it out too well, and your bone didn't make any of that sandy stuff." He didn't leave much room for optimism; my mom had to wait two more weeks to see if the bone began to heal. If it didn't, she would need a bone graft.

Understandably grumpy, she turned to her best antidote for discouragement: hiking. She called her friend Amy to pick a time and a trail. Since my mom still had her arm in a sling, they decided to forgo their usual rigorous routes and instead walked along a dirt path with only a slight incline. My mom later told me, "We weren't hiking with any dogs that day. There weren't any other people on the trail. Amy was in front of me, and I was hiking behind her." She likes to establish all those details before explaining what happened next. "All of a sudden, I felt someone push me. I got *shoved*. And I fell over sideways on the trail—right on my broken arm! It hurt *so* badly!" Although she knew she hadn't tripped, they checked the trail for roots, sticks, and rocks, and found nothing but dirt. My mom didn't see anyone but literally felt someone push her over and couldn't explain it.

For two days, she tried to ignore the increased pain in her arm but finally went back to the doctor in distress. He found that the plate and screws had kept the bone in place, but the impact had disturbed the bone enough to activate the production of callus, "the sandy stuff" that would glue it back together. Several weeks later, my mom's arm had healed, and she did not need a bone graft. I had believed in guardian angels my whole life, visualizing them gently ministering to us and watching over us. It made me smile to picture how my adventurous, down-to-earth mom must have a "tough love" kind of guardian angel who will give her an abrupt shove if that is the only way to deliver the blessing she needs.

* * *

The Holy Ghost might not deliver messages to you in the form of powerful feelings or dramatic experiences. Instead, you might get an idea that doesn't seem connected to your current train of thought. My sister, Sadie, half-jokingly claims, "The Holy Ghost lives at the grocery store—or at least, visits there often." As she walks from aisle to aisle, gathering ingredients for various recipes, she frequently thinks of an item that is not on her grocery list. Immediately, my frugal sister dismisses the idea, telling herself, "I don't need that for any of the dinners I have planned," or, "I just bought that last week." Often, the item that pops into her mind is perishable or something she uses less frequently than the regular staples, like fresh mushrooms or a can of coconut milk.

Later in the week, Sadie will have a thought to double a recipe so she can take some to a neighbor but will quickly realize that to make a larger amount, she would need the can of coconut milk she chose not to purchase. Another time, a friend might reach out and ask if Sadie has any mushrooms and she will immediately remember standing in the store, thinking about grabbing some mushrooms and deciding against it. You know how your week unfolds with surprises. A friend stays for dinner. A teenager uses up the last of a favorite condiment and forgets to tell anyone. You get distracted and fail to take something out of the freezer in time. Dozens of these kinds of situations left Sadie wishing she paid closer attention to the ideas she gets about groceries, although they never feel like promptings. She finally resolved to let go of her list long enough to listen.

* * *

One of the most beautiful and fascinating aspects of inspiration is how it can range in scope, significance, and subject matter. What a gift to know that God loves us enough to send messages about both the critical and incidental parts of our lives! President Nelson testified, "If we will truly receive the Holy Ghost and learn to discern and understand His promptings, we will be guided in matters large and small."[30] Thankfully, once we choose to believe that our Heavenly Parents might occasionally care about our grocery lists, we can receive inspiration about more serious situations.

Seventeen years ago, a few of my former coworkers met for lunch. Though we came from different cultural backgrounds, including Greek, Japanese, and Brazilian, we had the gospel of Jesus Christ in common. Without the constraints of cubicles or software development deadlines, we began to talk about tender mercies. Soon, we discovered a shared passion for noticing miracles of all sizes in our ordinary lives. As we continued to meet for lunch over the years, the unspoken agenda for these reunions always included stories of tested faith, answered prayers, and moments that put oil in our lamps.

We all took turns sharing, but everyone had the same favorite storyteller: Plinio Pimentel. Buoyant and expressive, Plinio travels extensively and seems to attract and spread miracles like a bee redistributes pollen. At one lunch, he surprised us with the news that his wife, Felicia, had received an unmistakable impression to quit her job teaching advanced placement English to high school students. As an "empty nester," she couldn't fathom why God would direct her to abruptly end her employment when Plinio still worked full-time and their three adult children all had busy lives of their own. Even though it didn't make sense to her, Felicia obeyed the instruction that she believed came from the Lord.

Several months after Felicia quit, their oldest daughter, Paula, started having debilitating headaches. With Paula's husband at work during the day, Felicia began to help Paula care for their toddler and baby. Even though Dexter, Paula's husband, did as much as he could during the evenings and his parents and many other people provided

---

30. Russell M. Nelson, "Revelation for the Church, Revelation for Our Lives," *Ensign*, May 2018.

countless hours of service, Felicia felt grateful to be available to help her daughter in ways that her teaching schedule would not have allowed.

Plinio stopped for a bite of food as we marveled at the way Felicia listened to the Spirit and retired just in time to serve her family in such a significant way. But his story continued to unfold. The headaches continued for months, and finally doctors diagnosed Paula with a spontaneous cerebrospinal fluid leak. They prescribed blood patches, injecting Paula's own blood around her spine to try to stop the leak, but unfortunately, the resulting relief only lasted for a week or two at a time. Finally, her doctors referred her to a neurosurgeon in Los Angeles who had developed a procedure using high quality MRI imaging to identify the location of the leaks and then repair the tears or holes with surgery.

Plinio planned to fly with Paula to California so that Dexter could be home with their kids at night. Felicia continued to help take care of the kids during the day as she had done for the previous six months. As they waited to find out if the insurance company would cover the cost of the procedure, family and friends prayed and fasted. Plinio fasted for two days straight. When the news came that the insurance company would pay for the surgery, everyone felt optimistic that the trip to Los Angeles would bring an end to Paula's suffering.

Unfortunately, the medical team could not locate the leak that caused the excruciating headaches. Even after multiple days of MRI imaging, nothing showed up on the scans. When Plinio and Paula met with the neurosurgeon to discuss the situation, he had devastating news. They would have to cancel the surgery.

Suddenly, a clear thought came into Plinio's mind, and he knew the location of the spinal fluid leak. As the Spirit gave to him "in the very hour, yea, in the very moment"[31] what to say, Plinio announced that the leak was located between the lower vertebrae. No one had even mentioned that possibility. Since most spontaneous spinal fluid leaks occur in the middle spine or higher,[32] the specialized equipment had only scanned Paula's upper back and neck. But the Holy Ghost

31. Doctrine and Covenants 100:6.
32. "Spinal Fluid Leak," Columbia Neruosurgery, https://www.neurosurgery.columbia.edu/patient-care/conditions/spinal-fluid-leak.

enabled Plinio to remember a tiny detail which no one at that hospital knew, information he had previously deemed unimportant and forgotten: the blood patch that had given Paula the most days of relief had been injected between her lower vertebrae.

Plinio boldly recommended that the medical team perform surgery on Paula the next day without doing additional expensive imaging. The doctor listened carefully, then agreed to do the procedure. The following morning, he discovered a patch of membrane so thin that it seeped out spinal fluid "like a wet tea bag," as Paula described later. That extremely thin patch of dura would not have shown up on a scan. He also found and fixed another hidden leak, completing a miraculous repair that cured Paula's headaches.

Plinio finished the story with his testimony that he had no doubts about the source of the idea that came to his mind. Like Felicia, he chose to recognize the origin of the impression he received. Although that stretch of their mortal journey felt long and painful for all the members of the Pimentel family, especially Paula, they believe that God led them through it. Their faith increased mine, as well as that of everyone at our lunch, where we were once again both physically and spiritually fed.

* * *

As we share our luminous stones with others, we can help them learn how to recognize the Holy Ghost. Your story might especially bless an individual who has heard many examples of only one way that people receive personal revelation. Vicki F. Matsumori, second counselor in the Primary General Presidency, taught: "We can help others become more familiar with the promptings of the Spirit when we share our testimony of the influence of the Holy Ghost in our lives. Remember that some experiences are too sacred to relate. However, by sharing testimony of the Spirit in our lives, those who are unfamiliar with these promptings are more likely to recognize when they have similar feelings."[33]

---

33. Vicki F. Matsumori "Helping Others Recognize the Whisperings of the Spirit" *Ensign*, November 2009.

God has sent messages—and messengers—to you through the Holy Ghost. When have you noticed the hand of God in your life? You can respond to one or more of the starter questions on the lined pages at the end of this chapter.

The next four chapters each focus on one type of personal revelation:

- Moments when we feel God's love
- Answers we get to our prayers
- Promptings we receive
- Experiences that build our faith

Many of your spiritual experiences might fit into more than one of these categories, since they naturally overlap, and one might function as a catalyst for another.

When did you most recently feel the Spirit?

____

____

____

____

____

____

Does the Holy Ghost primarily communicate with you through thoughts or feelings?

____

____

____

____

____

____

Has the Spirit ever delivered a message to you in another way?

____

____

____

____

____

____

CHAPTER 3
Feeling Loved

Along with the peaceful direction we receive from the Holy Ghost, from time to time, God powerfully and very personally assures each of us that He knows us and loves us and that He is blessing us specifically and openly.[34]

—Elder Neil L. Andersen

For many people, the initial message they receive from heaven is a sense that God knows and loves them. Later, we learn how to obtain guidance and follow impressions. But first, the Holy Ghost conveys the love of our Heavenly Parents and Jesus Christ to our hearts and minds. You might feel Their love through music, while in nature, or in quiet moments of reflection. Elder David A. Bednar shared:

> A loving Savior was sending me a most personal and timely message of comfort and reassurance through a hymn selected weeks previously. Some may count this experience as simply a nice coincidence, but I testify that the tender mercies of the Lord are real and that they do not occur randomly or merely by coincidence. Often, the Lord's timing of His tender mercies helps us to both discern and acknowledge them.[35]

---

34. Neil L. Andersen, "Spiritually Defining Memories" *Ensign*, May 2020.
35. David A. Bednar, "The Tender Mercies of the Lord" *Ensign*, May 2005.

I first learned of tender mercies in my own family as I sat with my cousins on the floor by the crackling fireplace at a family Christmas party. My grandpa welcomed everyone to his home and expressed joy that so many of his children and grandchildren could gather to celebrate together. Then, he told us that before we ate, he wanted to share a story from his father's missionary journal. My great-grandfather, Edward LaVaun Clissold, served a full-time mission in 1921 at the age of twenty-three. Even though he left behind a pregnant wife, he served as a missionary in Hawaii for three years. Perhaps their willingness to sacrifice for the Lord explains the tender mercy he recorded in his journal:

> We left before the sun came up and walked for several miles along the beach toward the little town of Punaluu. The drinking water at Hapai's was partly brackish and it was difficult to quench our thirst completely. As we walked along in the heat of the rising sun, I became very thirsty and mentioned it to Elder Weaver. He agreed that it was hot and that we had a long distance to go before we would get any relief. We finally left the seashore and cut up over the lava plateau toward Naalehu.
>
> As we walked my thirst increased and I finally decided that nothing would quench it but an orange. I repeated this to Elder Weaver several times and finally he became a little irritated and said, "Why do you keep talking of oranges? There is no possibility of finding an orange tree in this desert!" Finally, we went through a fence and in the distance saw a watering trough for cattle. I thought here at last was the possibility of quenching our thirst. As we approached the trough, I noticed some yellow object on a board that partly covered it. I fixed my eye on this object and as we came closer and closer, I realized that I was looking at several oranges.
>
> Brother Weaver said, "What in the world is this? I can't believe my eyes!" We took the oranges. They were not even warm from the sun and were fresh. As I peeled one, the thought occurred to me, "Why would we have oranges and water at the same place?" Then, upon examining the water trough, I found that the outlet from the pipe coming down over the plateau into the trough was tightly boarded up to

protect it from breakage by the cattle, leaving available only water unfit for human consumption.

We ate the fruit and went on our way, rejoicing.[36]

As he concluded, my grandpa emphasized with tears in his eyes that no one can explain how the fruit got there or why it still felt cool to the touch. He said that his father looked in every direction but couldn't find anyone who could have delivered the oranges. Later, my grandpa told me that type of orange was not indigenous to the island.

Hearing the story of my thirsty ancestor and the oranges left an impression on my soul that never faded. I understand why Abraham said, "I shall endeavor to write some of these things upon this record, for the benefit of my posterity that shall come after me."[37] The account recorded by my great-grandfather one hundred years ago helps me remember that someone in our family experienced physical evidence of God's awareness. Because I shared a fairly uncommon last name with the protagonist of the story, it impacted my testimony on a different level than even my favorite stories from the scriptures. My gratitude grew into a desire to preserve stories that would help my great-grandchildren feel the love of God someday.

Starters

- When have you felt the love of your Heavenly Parents?
- Have you ever had a moment when you could sense the love that God has for someone else?
- Have you ever received a priesthood blessing? Why did you get a blessing at that time? How did you feel during the blessing? Did the blessing help you?
- When have you felt like you have a relationship with Jesus Christ?
- Has the Holy Ghost ever guided you in how to be a more

---

36. Edward L. Clissold, "Assignment to Kona" https://www.familysearch.org/tree/person/memories/MB6X-B7B.
37. Abraham 1:31.

loving spouse or how to show more love as a parent, son, or daughter?

Stories

After my friend Yuki joined the Church and graduated from high school, she moved from Japan to Utah to go to college. Because she didn't have a car, she rode a blue bike all over campus. One day, Jim saw Yuki riding her bike. He could not stop thinking about "the girl on the bike," as he called her. A week later, he saw her walk into the bowling alley where he worked. He approached her and, since he had never seen her without it, asked, "Do you have a blue bike?" She had never heard anyone start a conversation that way. Not long after his memorable opening line, Jim and Yuki fell in love.

When they got engaged, Yuki coordinated the date with her parents, who planned to fly to Utah for the wedding day, even though they could not attend the temple sealing. Yuki's father had not joined the Church, and her mother did not have a temple recommend. But Yuki looked forward to seeing them and felt blessed that they could celebrate with her on her important day. Going to school full-time and planning a wedding in a foreign country without any family in town kept her busy during the weeks leading up to the wedding.

Just before her parents left Japan, they called with wonderful news. Yuki's mother had obtained a temple recommend and could go to Jim's and Yuki's sealing! Although her mom didn't speak English, Yuki felt thrilled that she would be in the room with them to witness the ceremony. She knew that her mom would feel the Spirit even if she couldn't understand the words the sealer would say.

On their wedding day, they sat together in a small, bright room that sparkled with chandelier crystals and spotless mirrors. The sealer, whom Jim and Yuki had not met before that morning, welcomed everyone warmly. After talking with them for a moment, he smiled and said, "Many years ago, I served a mission in Japan." He proceeded to give wonderful words of counsel, saying each sentence twice, once in English and once in Japanese. As he pronounced the beautiful blessings upon Jim and Yuki in both languages, Yuki felt Heavenly Father's love for all of them. Later, she found out that during the sealing ceremony, as her father sat by himself in the marriage waiting area, the temple president met and visited with him there. God knew where in the temple to send each of His servants that day.

* * *

One of the best feelings in the world comes from the realization that Jesus Christ knows exactly where you are and what you need in that moment. He can supply miracles for us that no one else can provide. From our earliest days on earth, when someone meets our needs, especially our unspoken needs, we feel dearly loved. Yuki and I have both experienced moments when we felt that our Savior walked ahead of us and prepared a blessing for us to discover.

When my former husband and I separated and began the painful process of divorce, he told me that he didn't plan to take any of our furniture. I had assumed we would divide our belongings, but he pointed out the benefit to our kids of having an unaltered environment at my house instead of having both of their homes change. I stayed in our house, and he bought the house directly behind it. We made one section of the fence into a gate so our kids could go back and forth through the backyards. I appreciated the selfless way he walked away from all the furnishings we had collected, purchased, and received as gifts over thirteen years of marriage to give our young kids an extra portion of stability. He took only his clothing and some dishes and set out to fill his new home from scratch.

An extremely avid outdoorsman, he had always spent his free time hunting, camping, and fishing, so I wasn't surprised when his first few decorations included wooden trout wall hangings and a colorful print of a moose. Those minor purchases brightened empty walls and made the house feel homey. But after a few weeks, it hit me that he would be getting all new furniture, while I would still have all the old furniture. I didn't question his stated motive, but I started to feel slightly resentful because we hadn't yet divided our finances and he ordered his new furniture on our joint credit card. If I could have accessed the logical part of my brain, it would have pointed out how we didn't have another credit card and how I didn't have a job. But logical thought lay trapped under layers of hurt feelings.

I began to look at my old dining room table with new eyes. Scratched and dented, it bore plenty of kid-inflicted fork scars. I had always liked how the solid, round tabletop meant that everyone sat facing the whole family, with no one at the "head" of the table. A couple in my parents' neighborhood had given it to us, and it fit well in our small dining room. But now, it just looked dirty and hammered. That table became a symbol for everything in my life that seemed unfair.

One day, the kids came back to my house talking about their new leather sectional with three different footrests that popped up when they pulled a lever. They clearly loved it, and once again, I felt the secret jealousy growing larger in my chest. The worn fabric couch in my basement had belonged to my in-laws for more than a decade before we inherited it. It didn't quite fit in the room, so we had chopped it shorter with a saw and stapled the worn upholstery over the raw edge. "Dad's house" had novelty and a fresh start with no stacks of old papers, no cheap kids' meal toys cluttering the dresser tops, and no secondhand furniture.

Weeks passed, and I heard that he had ordered a new dining room table from Pottery Barn, a high-end furniture store where we had never shopped as a couple. While I understood the value of investing in something that would last, I felt consumed with the unfair circumstances. I didn't want to feel bitter about the situation or angry with the father of my children, so I directed my resentment toward the unseen inanimate object on its way to my children's new home. Every time I walked back to my house, everything looked worn out, the way my heart felt. I dreaded the day when I had to see his new table. While I prayed for the capacity to move past these petty emotions, I knew it would take time and mental effort to feel content with what I had.

Then, an incredibly tender mercy occurred and became one of the purest luminous stones of my life—a simple moment where I felt complete love and understanding from God. It came in an ordinary way, as I sat in an ordinary church classroom. Our Gospel Doctrine teacher, Don Glenn, asked someone to read out loud from the Old Testament. I listened as a member of my ward family read:

> And Abram went up out of Egypt, he and his wife, and all that he had, and Lot with him, into the south. And Abram was very rich in cattle, in silver, and in gold.

> And Lot also, which went with Abram, had flocks, and herds, and tents. And the land was not able to bear them, that they might dwell together for their substance was great, so that they could not dwell together.
>
> And Abram said unto Lot, Let there be no strife, I pray thee, between me and thee, and between my herdsmen and thy herdsmen; for we be brethren. Is not the whole land before thee? Separate thyself, I pray thee, from me if thou wilt take the left hand, then I will go the right; or if thou depart to the right hand, then I will go to the left.[38]

I sat in stunned tears. What were the odds that we would discuss Genesis 13 that week? How many times in the Old Testament do people divide their belongings? Whispering, I reread the words "they could not dwell together," and I wept. I felt my Heavenly Parents speaking to me through those scriptures, which acted as a conduit for great comfort. "Let there be no strife," I repeated to myself. Basking in divine love made material possessions seem unimportant. I sat in Sunday School, and Jesus Christ healed my heart.

Relieved and rejuvenated, I spent several glorious days without a single thought about anyone's dining room table. Then, one evening, I walked over to my former husband's house to help the kids feed and kennel the dogs because he had gone out of town. As they opened the sliding glass door to fill up the water dish at the kitchen sink, I suddenly saw it.

The new table.

Smooth and sturdy, the wood gleamed in the afternoon sunshine. The table itself didn't surprise me; I had anticipated a beautiful grain and a contemporary color. The unexpected part sat next to the table: instead of dining room chairs, I saw a bench. I checked the other side—two benches, like a picnic table at a campsite! And as I looked at them, I noticed a shocking absence of jealousy. The Sunday School discussion had softened my heart, making room for grace.

I said to myself, "It looks just like him!" My eyes filled with happy tears at how the table and benches reflected his passion for the outdoors. It seemed perfect for his new house as he started his own life

---

38. Genesis 13: 1, 5–6, 8–9.

with our kids. I knew how hard he worked to make them feel comfortable there and how much energy he dedicated to creating a unique family culture with new traditions and routines. As I looked at that table, I didn't think about the price, the brand, or how it compared to my table. I felt no jealousy, no resentment; I felt nothing that hurt my heart! The one object that I had obsessed over brought me joy instead of bitterness. That dining room table became a gift from God to me, a gift that made me feel abundantly loved.

* * *

The scriptures are full of stories in which one of God's children has a spiritual experience that involves a physical object. We live in such a tangible, concrete world, and God seems to understand that physical objects and actions help us learn, remember, and make promises. Miraculously, everyday items often become vehicles for God's love and light. In Ether 3, we read:

> And it came to pass that the brother of Jared . . . went forth unto the mount . . . and did molten out of a rock sixteen small stones; and they were white and clear, even as transparent glass; and he did carry them in his hands upon the top of the mount, and cried again unto the Lord, saying. . . . I know, O Lord, that thou hast all power and can do whatsoever thou wilt for the benefit of man; therefore touch these stones, O Lord, with thy finger, and prepare them that they may shine forth in darkness.[39]

I love that he carried the rocks "in his hands." Perhaps pockets had not yet been invented. More likely, he did not want to stash those important stones in any kind of a pouch and chose instead to carefully cradle them on his way to present them to the Lord. In the same way Jesus Christ infused those sixteen stones with light, He infused a table with His love. Many of His ancient miracles involved objects as ordinary as

39. Ether 3:1, 4.

water and dirt. If we watch carefully, we will see how the Savior still uses seemingly insignificant items to execute modern-day miracles.

When Shelley McConkie's husband received a call to serve as a stake president, they had six kids under the age of twelve—and one on the way. She told me that she felt like a "deer in headlights" for months as she processed the probable impacts of this new calling on their family. She confided, "I felt so overwhelmed when I thought about how, by the time he got released, our unborn baby would be in fourth grade! And for our five-year old, this calling would basically last the rest of his childhood!" But despite a myriad of emotions, Matthew and Shelley moved forward with faith, serving with great compassion and humility.

As stake conference approached, the wife of one of Matthew's counselors approached Shelley with an idea. She suggested that they buy new ties for their husbands to wear to each stake conference during their tenure together. Shelley loved the thoughtful plan and agreed to participate. But seven children filled her days with tasks and errands, and soon the special weekend arrived. The night before the conference, Shelley frantically ran through the mall, trying to find the right tie to commemorate her husband's first stake conference as president. She later said, "All of the cheap ties were ugly! And the good ones cost eighty dollars! I got more and more discouraged until I ran out of time. Finally, I left the mall without a tie."

Feeling defeated, Shelley sat in the meeting and stewed over how she had not completed her goal. Not only had she failed to celebrate this first stake conference with a special gift, but she had also missed the opportunity to join the others as they started a tradition. When her husband stood at the pulpit and spoke eloquently about the Savior's admonition to "feed my sheep," her heart felt heavy with her inability to serve her spouse in a small way.

After everyone said "amen" to the closing prayer, members of the stake stood up and began to greet each other in the pews and aisles of the chapel. As Shelley visited with neighbors, a man walked up and told her, "I gave your husband my tie." Shelley stared at him in disbelief.

"What? You did what?"

"I gave him my tie. His talk was about 'feed my sheep,' and I was wearing a tie with sheep on it, so I gave it to him. I told him that he should take off his tie and put on mine."

At that moment, Shelley felt like God was telling her, "I've got your back." She knew that He saw her and loved her. She later wrote:

> The statistical improbability of both a sheep tie and someone willing to take it off their neck and give it away was not lost on me. The only logical explanation was simply this: God was telling me He was aware of me and the unspoken desires of my heart. He was aware of all the things I wanted to do but was having a hard time doing because #life. And He was telling me that He would send people to help me.

The man that God sent that morning was Ron Radcliffe. While not an official member of the Church, Ron occasionally attended meetings with his wife, Judy, a longtime member. When Ron heard President McConkie's message on service, the Spirit touched his heart. He had no way of knowing what his impromptu gift would mean to Shelley, but he followed through on a generous and unconventional idea that came into his mind.

Ron didn't stop with that act of service. At the beginning of stake conference weekend six months later, Matthew and Shelley heard the doorbell ring. When they opened their front door, they found a brown paper bag on their front porch. No tag or note accompanied the gift, but a hand-drawn sheep on the front confirmed their suspicions. Inside, they found a beautiful new tie. And for the last four years, Ron has left a new tie on their porch before each stake conference, a physical reminder of God's awareness and the way He often meets our needs through others.

* * *

Sometimes, we see God's hand clearly and immediately, but often we don't recognize events as manifestations of God's love until much later. As a single mom, each month I put any extra money that I had toward paying down my car loan so I could get out of debt. Only once did I deviate from my personal policy, and at the time, I didn't recognize a prompting. It started when I got a letter in the mail that sounded like a scam. Asking me to confirm my address by calling a phone number, the letter claimed that this company wanted to send some money to me. I showed the letter to my former husband and asked him what he thought. Luckily, he recognized the name of the company and told me, "Remember that software company you worked for back in 2000? This is the company that bought them. They are saying that you had some shares, and they want to pay you for them." I had completely forgotten that my initial compensation package included a modest number of shares in that small company. I called and confirmed my mailing address, unsure of how much money they would send if I ever heard from them again.

To my surprise and delight, a check arrived in the mail for $1,500, a substantial amount for a single mom who worked from home at night as a technical writer. I didn't make much money and relied on the generous alimony and child support that my former husband provided so that I could stay at home with our kids. Although I used rebates, birthday checks (don't tell my grandparents), and income from freelance work to pay off my car faster, I did not do the same with the unexpected $1,500. Instead, I deposited it into my savings account. I didn't get instructions in my mind from the Holy Ghost or experience a strong feeling; I just decided that I should hang onto that money, and I didn't know why.

A couple of months later, I reached out to my friend Jeff to ask him for advice about the freelance writing company that I had recently started. I needed to figure out how to pay a subcontractor and knew that he ran a couple of businesses. Offering to send me some resources, he asked for my email address. I spelled it out, "R-u-k-a- . . . " and he sounded intrigued.

"I know your last name," he said, referring to part of my email address. "But what is Ruka?" Because I love the story and memories behind it, I eagerly explained the history of my unusual nickname.

"When I worked as a counselor at a girl's camp during the summer of 1997, everyone had to pick a camp name, like Sunshine or Aspen. I wanted to find a unique counselor nickname, so I went to the library and used an English-Swahili dictionary to look up words until I found one that I liked. I looked up the word for 'dance' because I love to dance, and it said that 'rukaruka' means 'to jump, to dance.' I thought a four-syllable word seemed too long for a camp name, so I shortened it to just Ruka, and I went by that all summer. I still have a lot of friends from camp that call me Ruka instead of Rachel."

"That's fun. But why did you want to find a Swahili word?" Jeff asked.

"Because if I could travel anywhere in the world, I would go to Kenya. It's been my number-one dream to go there and see the elephants ever since I was in high school. I even have this big plastic jar in my laundry room, and I wrote 'Africa' on it with a Sharpie fourteen years ago, and I have been putting my loose change in it ever since!"

Even though I tend to overshare, I wasn't sure why I told Jeff these random pieces of information. The poor man hadn't asked for a free association glimpse into my brain! I had more that I could have mentioned, like how my grandparents had friends from Kenya when I was growing up and the Kalui family used to come to our family parties. Or how a Kenyan student named Eddie became my first international pen pal, and we wrote letters back and forth for years. I didn't tell Jeff that I blasted the song "Jambo Bwana" in my car every day when I drove kindergarten carpool. I didn't get a chance to tell Jeff any of those connections because to my surprise, he told me, "I am going to Kenya next month."

Without even thinking, I blurted, "I want to go to Kenya next month!" I only said it as a statement of fact, not a request; I couldn't have imagined it as a real possibility. I said it the way people wish out loud for a million dollars. But his reply left me completely stunned.

"Would you be interested in joining us if I could get permission to add you to the group?" He explained that his company had raised money to build a school in a village called Boyani and that a group of employees and their family members planned to attend the groundbreaking and deliver medical and school supplies.

"I would do anything to go to Kenya! I would find someone to watch my kids! I would figure out how to make it happen!"

Jeff offered to ask the executive team the next day, although I couldn't imagine how they might have a spot left on such short notice when they had been planning the trip for over a year. Not wanting to get my hopes up, Jeff reminded me that even if they agreed, I would still need vaccinations, supplies, and an expedited passport, all in a matter of three weeks. He promised to call me the next day.

Although I felt sure that my non-employee status would render me ineligible, my heart still pounded when I saw his name on my phone. Then, he said the words I will never forget. "Great news! It turns out, there are only five women going on the trip, but they are going to sleep on bunk beds, so there is an extra bed! And we had too many people for two vans, but we don't fill up three. So, we can provide your lodging and transportation in Kenya without any additional cost to the company." Before I could interject, he added, "You would have to pay for your malaria and yellow fever shots, which cost three hundred dollars. And you would need to cover your own airfare. I looked up the current rates and your plane ticket would be twelve hundred dollars."

My heart and eyes filled up and spilled over simultaneously. Jeff didn't know about my shares in the software company. He didn't know that I had that exact amount just sitting in my account. He didn't know how easily I could have put that $1,500 toward my car and not had any extra money on hand. But when I told him, he sounded amazed at the growing number of synchronicities. We both felt like God wanted me to go to Kenya

When I traveled with Jeff and his coworkers to Boyani, I felt like my Heavenly Parents had given me the most loving, personalized tender mercy in the world. I felt happier and more myself than I had felt since my divorce. Having a faraway adventure like that, fulfilling a longtime dream, and serving my brothers and sisters in Africa convinced my subconscious that I would be okay on my own and that I could have a great life, even though it wouldn't match the original plans I had made. Clearly, the unexpected check in the mail, the extra bunk bed, and the fact that Jeff's company chose the same country I had dreamed of visiting did not constitute a series of mere coincidences. But when I assumed that my trip to Kenya was the ultimate compensatory blessing, I underestimated what the Lord can imagine and orchestrate.

Because a year after we went to Kenya together, Jeff and I got married.

* * *

When have you felt God's love flow into your life? When have you felt seen and cared for by Him? The next few pages contain the starters from this chapter, along with room for you to jot down your thoughts. You may use the extra pages for experiences that don't quite fit any of these prompts.

When have you felt the love of your Heavenly Parents?

Have you ever had a moment when you could sense the love that God has for someone else?

Have you ever received a priesthood blessing? Why did you get a blessing at that time?

How did you feel during the blessing? Did the blessing help you?

When have you felt like you have a relationship with Jesus Christ?

Has the Holy Ghost ever guided you in how to be a more loving spouse or how to show more love as a parent, son, or daughter?

CHAPTER 4

Receiving Answers

The ability to qualify for, receive, and act on personal revelation is the single most important skill that can be acquired in this life. . . . Promised personal revelation comes when we ask for it, prepare for it, and go forward in faith, trusting that it will be poured out upon us.[40]

—President Julie B. Beck

When we take questions to God through prayer, we demonstrate faith that we will receive an answer. Every volume of scripture supports this expectation, from the ancient teaching, "Whatsoever ye shall ask, it shall be given you,"[41] to the modern-day revelation that echoes it, "It shall be given you what you shall ask."[42] Jesus Christ Himself taught the Nephites, "Whatsoever things ye shall ask the Father in my name shall be given unto you."[43]

For years, when I testified about the power of prayer, I said, "Answers to prayer don't always come the way we expect." But as I have gotten older, I have changed my statement to, "Answers to prayer

---

40. Julie B. Beck, "And Upon the Handmaids in Those Days Will I Pour out My Spirit," *Ensign*, May 2010.
41. Moses 6:52.
42. Doctrine and Covenants 50:30.
43. 3 Nephi 27:28.

don't *usually* come the way we expect!" Once or twice in a lifetime, you might wish for oranges and get oranges. But more often, you will get mangoes or pineapple or an opportunity to hike to a faraway natural spring. Answers arrive in diverse ways and at different times than we picture in our minds.

One Sunday, I substituted a youth Sunday School class in our ward. During the discussion, I asked the teenagers if any of them would share a personal example about prayer. "It could be about anything at all!" I encouraged. "Any time that you prayed about anything and got *any* kind of an answer." Genuinely curious about how they might respond, I had been looking forward to asking this question. Kennedy, a junior in high school, raised her hand and I almost clapped at her bravery. But ultimately, her answer deserved applause even more than her courage did. Almost offhandedly, she said in her deep alto voice, "I prayed about my AP physics test . . . "

Before she could continue, one of the boys interrupted to ask, "Did you pass it?"

In an advanced placement (AP) class, high school students must earn at least a three out of five on the end-of-year test to earn college credit. Kennedy quickly admitted, "No, I bombed it." Everyone laughed, including Kennedy, but then she added in her down-to-earth way, "But I didn't feel super upset about it, so I think that was an answer to my prayer!" I loved her attitude and her faith.

When answers do arrive in the way we had hoped, we can carefully record those experiences and use them to bolster our faith on the days when answers take more time and patience. Though we might feel confident that we know what is best for us, we still operate with a limited perspective. I once heard a memorable testimony from a young father who sat on the back row of our chapel. Just starting their parenthood adventure, Mark and Angie had a two-year-old they called Scottie. Mark told our ward the struggle they had to get Scottie to eat any food other than blue yogurt. Scottie wanted to consume nothing but blue yogurt from a squeezable plastic tube at every single meal. Mark tearfully testified that he had received a glimpse into how Heavenly Father must feel when we beg for certain blessings and He has a better plan for us. Mark said he knew how badly Scottie wanted that yogurt but also knew that a variety of foods would nourish his little body much better. Mark wondered out loud how many times he has asked God for more blue yogurt.

Often it takes both hindsight and faith to see how God's ideas and plans far exceed our own. Such realizations become priceless testimony builders for us and others when we write them down, even in the simplest, most straightforward way. As our children hear our stories, they will learn to trust in our Heavenly Parents' creativity, wisdom, and love.

Starters

- When have you prayed for help and felt like you received some form of assistance from heaven, either from another person, something you read in the scriptures, or a feeling or thought that came to you?
- Have you ever received an idea about what to do in your Church calling?
- Have you ever received comfort or inspiration about a particularly difficult relationship? What happened?
- What is the most unusual place where you received an answer to a prayer?

Stories

Ed and Dinah spent the entire summer preparing for their daughter's wedding reception, which they planned to host on their family's property in the mountains. With a small pond and sprawling willow trees, the spot provided a beautiful backdrop but needed a lot of work. Ed moved around a sprinkler for weeks to help the grass stay green as the summer got hotter. Then he mowed the adjacent field to create a makeshift parking lot for wedding guests. Dinah planted wildflowers in pots for centerpieces, rented plastic tables and chairs, and worked with a caterer to design a simple buffet dinner, since everyone who attended would have a long drive up and down the canyon.

After consulting an almanac, Ed and Dinah felt safe planning an outdoor reception for late August and didn't create any kind of contingency plan for bad weather. The wedding day started with a clear, warm morning, but when the family walked out of the temple after the ceremony, dark clouds crowded the sky. As they arrived at the pond, they found the tables and chairs covered with water droplets. The rain persisted as a cold, steady drizzle, accompanied by a chilly wind that didn't seem compatible with lightweight rented tablecloths. No one dared plug in the extension cord connected to strands of tiny, white lights in the trees, and everyone worried about the live band that would soon arrive. Without a pavilion or tents, Ed and Dinah knew that the weather would ruin the celebration. No shelter existed within a mile other than a small mobile home that offered a single toilet and a kitchenette for the caterer. "The trailer," as the family called it, couldn't even accommodate the wedding party, let alone the hundreds of guests that planned to arrive an hour later.

As Ed walked across the green but soggy grass, Dinah intercepted him and poked him in the chest with her finger, as dead serious as he had seen her in a decade. "I want you to go into that trailer," she said firmly. "I don't care who you have to talk to or what you have to say, but don't come out until you can tell me that this storm is going to stop!"

He would never forget the look in her eyes. He later said, "I knew that she knew we could make that happen. I knew that she had the faith that it could be done." So, Ed went into the trailer, knelt down, and began to pray. Pouring out his heart, Ed expressed their belief that the Lord could change the weather, then shared his and Dinah's fervent desire that the wedding reception could happen the way their daughter hoped it would. After some time, Ed felt a confirmation that the Lord had heard his prayer. He walked out of the trailer to where Dinah stood and said with humble certainty, "Twenty minutes."

Relief wiped the worry lines from her forehead as he promised, "In twenty minutes, the weather will break." Unaware of their conversation, relatives patiently waited for instructions. Twenty minutes later, the rain stopped, and the dark clouds moved to the edges of the sky. The wind settled down as grandparents and cousins quickly dried off the folding chairs with towels. Dinah placed framed photos and flower pots on the tables. Someone plugged in the lights in the willow trees just as the guests parked their cars in the field.

The temperature went up by almost ten degrees as old friends and family members hugged, laughed, and talked. The bride, completely unaware of how the miracle occurred, beamed with joy as she danced outside with her favorite people. But more than anyone else, Ed and Dinah celebrated with immense relief and gratitude. Later, Ed reflected:

> The Lord had granted our petition and had blessed us that we could have a break in the weather so the reception could go off as planned. It was a literal, immediate answer to prayer and a miracle. I am so grateful to have been a part of that and to be able to witness that, to recognize the Lord's hand. He blessed what we had prepared and what we desired for that day. It was one of the great testimony builders that I have had in my life.

* * *

Sometimes, we tend to *under* pray, as if the Lord only has a fixed number of blessings to bestow. But when we strive to keep the commandments, "then shall [our] confidence wax strong in the presence of God."[44] The Bible Dictionary says:

> The object of prayer is not to change the will of God but to secure for ourselves and for others blessings that God is already willing to grant but that are made conditional on our asking for them. Blessings require some work or effort on our part before we can obtain them. Prayer is a form of work and is an appointed means for obtaining the highest of all blessings.

During an overwhelming trial in my life, I prayed with intensity for someone to consult about the complicated situation in which I found myself. I didn't have any friends who had experienced similar

---

44. Doctrine and Covenants 121:45.

problems and wasn't sure where to turn for advice. I admitted to Heavenly Father, "I don't know who to talk to about this!" I sincerely pleaded for this specific blessing, completely unsure how God would grant it. I had racked my brain for solutions, considering a wide range of relatives and acquaintances, but hadn't come up with any names.

That summer, I attended a Relief Society book club at a home in my neighborhood. The participants had committed to read one chapter of *Daughters in My Kingdom* and then meet to discuss it. As we began talking about the assigned reading, my good friend, Ruth, appeared in the doorway. She looked slightly apologetic and almost surprised at her own arrival. Late, flustered, and pointing to the visible dirt on her jeans, she exclaimed, "I was gardening! I wasn't going to come tonight. I didn't even read the book!" Everyone laughed and encouraged her to get some food before she sat down. Ruth went into the next room to get a plate of refreshments, and I followed her to say hello and give her a hug.

She immediately sensed my secret distress. I ended up sitting in the kitchen with her for an hour, pouring out my heart and feeling stunned to learn that she had experienced a similar trial. In the fifteen years of our friendship, I had never heard anything about her previous experience, but God knew that Ruth could empathize with me and sent her to help. Because she listened to a prompting from the Holy Ghost and didn't argue with the logic of it, I received understanding and love. Sharing that burden didn't solve my problems, but talking to someone who had survived a similar situation filled my aching heart with comfort and hope.

* * *

When Ed prayed for a change in the weather, he could picture the outcome he desperately desired. When I asked God for someone I could talk to, I knew exactly what I wanted and needed, so I prayed for a specific type of assistance. But sometimes, complicated situations and relationships leave us unsure of what to ask for in our prayers. When that happens, we can trust that God knows our needs and will send an answer we haven't even considered.

For several weeks, my young son, Bear, struggled with managing his frustration during our morning routine, becoming increasingly disrespectful to me as he got ready for school. One morning, he yelled at me and snapped at his sisters in such a mean tone that hours after I dropped off the kids at school, I still felt uneasy. Disappointed that I had allowed him to talk that way, I teared up as I tried to figure out how to alter this exhausting behavior. I decided that I would use an archaic form of punishment I had only seen on TV shows. When he came home from school, I would make him write sentences. I hoped if he had to write out respectful alternatives for every unkind thing he had said before I allowed him to play with his friends, it would teach him a better way to communicate and hopefully create a consequence that a fourth grader wouldn't want to repeat.

With his sisters at a friend's house or still at school, I would have a perfect opportunity for one-on-one time with Bear. Not owning a one-room schoolhouse chalkboard, I sharpened pencils and created a homemade worksheet by printing his rude sentences with plenty of space after each one for his elementary school handwriting. A few minutes before I knew Bear would be home, I knelt in my bedroom and prayed for inspiration on how to best handle this important disciplining moment.

Suddenly, the thought came into my mind that I should get out my family ordinance cards. I retrieved a stack of pink and blue cards that listed our ancestors' names and the temple ordinances that they needed. As I carried them to our dining room table, the Spirit guided me to spread out the cards and group them by last name, lining up the siblings under the parents and indenting them by generation. I didn't know why, but I followed every step the Holy Ghost gave me.

When Bear walked in, the cards covered more space on the table than my disciplinary activity. He asked, "What are you doing with these?" I gave him a brief "show and tell," explaining which cards represented people who had all their temple work done and which people still waited. Then, I showed him four cards and said, "These are yours. I am going to save them for you and in two years, when you get your temple recommend, you can go and be baptized for these men."

He held them and read the names, then asked how they were related to him. We opened the FamilySearch website on my phone, and I showed him exactly how he was related to each of the individuals. Then he took a pen and a piece of paper from the table, and we drew a tree that depicted his relationship to the men in our family line. The afternoon sunshine lit up our dining room as he held the cards up to his face and hugged them to his cheek. Then, he quietly said something to them. I could tell he was not talking to the cards but to the people.

After we had enjoyed this peaceful time together talking about family history, our ancestors, and the house of the Lord, the previous tension between us had completely disappeared. I calmly told him that he had hurt my feelings that morning by being disrespectful and that he needed to think of a better way he could have said all those things. Uncharacteristically, he agreed without arguing. He sat down and carefully wrote thoughtful sentences, then apologized for the way he had behaved.

Later, I thought about my original plan to immediately demand that he sit down and write out sentences as punishment. Instead, God answered my prayer by filling our afternoon with a loving atmosphere. I had never considered the possibility that my ten-year-old would have an interest in family history but felt abundantly blessed that this experience ignited a spark in his soul.

* * *

Regardless of whether the answers to our prayers match, exceed, or barely resemble our expectations, we can choose to acknowledge God for His goodness and mercy. Will we label our luminous stones as a "nice coincidence"[45] or deepen our faith by correctly identifying them as blessings?

Several years ago, my parents went on a motorcycle trip through Canada. Six couples drove in a caravan of BMW adventure bikes, each couple sharing a motorcycle. As they sped along at seventy miles an hour through the forest, my dad and mom rode the last bike in line, bringing up the rear. Suddenly, they spotted a deer on the hillside,

45. David A. Bednar, "The Tender Mercies of the Lord" *Ensign*, May 2005.

heading straight for the highway. At the same moment, they both realized that the deer would inevitably collide with their motorcycle. In a flash, a prompting illuminated my dad's mind, telling him to *not* slow down because without the forward momentum, the bike would tip over on impact.

Miraculously, he managed to maintain control of the motorcycle. As they hit the deer, its body whipped around and crashed into my mom's leg, breaking it in five places below the knee. My dad used every ounce of his strength to keep the bike upright and drive to a place where they could safely stop. Later, my mom said that she couldn't believe they didn't tip over. Even my dad wondered out loud if he could have kept the motorcycle from going down without some kind of unseen help. Despite the horrific pain my mom experienced, they felt incredibly blessed to be alive, considering what could have happened if the bike had crashed to the ground. At best, additional injuries would have occurred, and at worst, another vehicle could have killed them if the bike had slid into oncoming traffic.

That night, surgeons set my mom's leg with pins and a metal rod. Then angelic Mennonite women cared for my mom in the hospital. It took a couple of days for her to reach a pain level where she could stand to fly home, a journey she had to make alone while my dad drove the motorcycle back to Utah. She hates to travel by herself even when she is well and whole; flying alone with a serious injury sounded like a nightmare. But they didn't have any other options.

The day before her flight, as my mom rested in the hospital, my dad got a call from Dave, the executive secretary in their ward. During the time my dad served as the bishop, Dave had become an honorary member of our family. Because he didn't have any family in Utah, my parents invited Dave to dinner, included him on holidays, and treated him as one of their own. My dad told Dave about the motorcycle accident, and when he got to the part about my mom's flight home, Dave exclaimed, "That's probably why my flight got changed! I've been traveling all week on business, and I had a direct flight home, but it just got rerouted through Spokane." The flight numbers confirmed that Dave would be on the same flight as my worried and exhausted mom.

After my mom returned home, a friend from her ward named Susan called to check on her. As they were talking, Susan said, "Something strange happened when you were on your trip. On Sunday, the person who gave the closing prayer in sacrament meeting prayed for your safety." That didn't sound strange to my mom, although she appreciated it. Susan continued, "And then we went to Sunday School and someone else prayed that you would be safe on your trip. And in Relief Society, the sister who said the prayer asked that our bishop and his wife would be protected as they traveled." My mom marveled that people offered similar prayers during all three hours of church. Then, Susan added, "After we heard that you got in an accident, my husband told me that the man who prayed in the high priest group also prayed for you. And we found out that the child who prayed in Primary asked Heavenly Father to watch over you and keep you safe."

The day before the accident, many members of the Silver Creek Ward had prayed for my parents, asking again and again for the same specific blessing. When my mom and dad talk about the miracles they experienced on their motorcycle trip, they testify that God answered those prayers.

* * *

Hopefully, you can think of a time when you received an answer to prayer. The following pages have room for you to respond to the starters in this chapter. Additional blank pages follow for other stories that come to your mind.

When have you prayed for help and felt like you received assistance from heaven, either from another person, something you read in the scriptures, or a feeling or thought that came to you?

Have you ever received an idea about what to do in your Church calling?

Have you ever received comfort or inspiration about a particularly difficult relationship? What happened?

What is the most unusual place where you received an answer to a prayer?

CHAPTER 5
Following Promptings

I have also learned that properly recording spiritual impressions demonstrates to the Savior how much I treasure His direction. The simple practice of writing down spiritual thoughts and feelings greatly enhances the likelihood of receiving and recognizing additional promptings from the Holy Ghost.[46]

—Elder David A. Bednar

While answers follow questions, promptings can occur unexpectedly. At certain times in our lives, we receive clear instructions from heaven that urge us to act or to stop moving in our current direction. We get to choose how we will respond and whether we will respond at all. Sometimes, we don't even recognize that a thought came from the Holy Ghost, believing instead that it originated in our mind. Other times, as President Dallin H. Oaks has taught, a nudge to do something "contrary to our personal preference" provides "evidence of authenticity."[47] Just like miracles

---

46. David A. Bednar, "Because We Have Them Before Our Eyes" *Ensign*, May 2006.
47. Dallin H. Oaks, "How can I distinguish the difference between the promptings of the Holy Ghost and merely my own thoughts, preferences, or hunches?" *Ensign*, June 1983.

vary in magnitude, promptings and impressions can range from small suggestions to significant commands.

One morning, my dad stood in his workshop, gathering tools to take to his barn, a short jaunt down the hillside. Before he left, the thought came to him that he should take his cordless drill. He immediately dismissed the idea, reminding himself, "I don't need my drill for the work I'm going to do today." He left without the drill and went down to the barn. Hours later, as he repaired the horse stalls, he found himself wishing he had his drill. Although only a slight delay and small inconvenience resulted, he wondered if Heavenly Father had tried to send a message through the Holy Ghost to make his day a little more efficient. Resolving to pay closer attention to ideas like that in the future, my dad shared this simple story with my brother, James.

Several years later, James stood in his bathroom, getting ready for work. As he reached to put his toothbrush back in a drawer, he saw a tube of lip balm and thought, "I should take that ChapStick with me." He remembers consciously rubbing his lips together to check whether they felt dry. Concluding that he did not have chapped lips, he closed the drawer and headed down the stairs without the lip balm. Halfway down, he remembered our dad's story about the drill. In a literal and figurative pivot, James turned around and went back upstairs to grab the ChapStick and put it in his pocket.

After a typical morning, James finished his lunch at his desk and felt an unexpected and sudden twinge of pain as his bottom lip split open. He later said:

> It wasn't a big deal. I could have gone to the gas station and picked up some ChapStick. Or I could have just waited until I got home, and my lip would have taken a little longer to heal. But because I had the ChapStick, I felt like God just wanted to make my life a little easier. And maybe He was giving me an opportunity to learn to trust Him and giving me a chance to show that He can trust me to follow promptings. If I can learn how to respond to simple things, I will be able to receive messages about more important things.

The source—not the size—of a prompting qualifies it as revelation. Sometimes, heavenly communication resembles an avalanche; more often, it feels like exquisite, individual snowflakes. Sydney S. Reynolds, first counselor in the Primary General Presidency, explained, "Just as important as these 'mighty miracles' are the smaller 'private miracles' that teach each of us to have faith in the Lord. These come as we recognize and heed the promptings of the Spirit in our lives."[48] Any message from God that you recognize as such can become a faith-building experience, regardless of the subject matter. The following starter questions focus on moments when you received specific directions from the Lord.

Starters

- When have you been an instrument in the hands of the Lord to answer someone else's prayer?
- Have you ever acted on a prompting to talk to someone whom you would not have approached on your own? What happened?
- When have you received direction from the Spirit that you knew was not from your own mind because it was something that you didn't want to do?
- Has the Holy Ghost ever delivered a message to you of correction or chastisement or showed you an area of weakness to help you repent?
- Have you ever followed a warning from the Holy Ghost that protected you from potential danger? What was the outcome?

Stories

Jeff didn't know why he felt prompted to attend the priesthood session of stake conference. He typically didn't attend *any* session of what he considered a semi-annual "weekend off" from church callings and responsibilities. When his ward leaders had announced the early-morning meeting the week before, participating hadn't crossed his mind, partly because no one would know if he attended. But, to

48. Sydney S. Reynolds, "A God of Miracles," *Ensign*, May 2001.

his surprise, he found himself getting dressed and driving to the stake center at 7:00 a.m., leaving two sleeping teenagers at home.

As he drove, he thought about the circumstances in his life that seemed far from ideal. His wife had stopped attending church several years earlier, and taking his kids by himself felt discouraging and lonely. She was currently on the other side of the country and had recently told Jeff that she did not want their marriage of twenty-seven years to continue. Several serious issues made divorce seem inevitable to everyone who knew them, but Jeff refused to accept it. Despondently, he walked into the chapel and sat on a bench a few rows from the front, still unsure why he felt compelled to attend.

Elder Ronald A. Rasband, then a member of the Presidency of the Seventy, presided at the meeting, and the program indicated that he would give some concluding comments. The last speaker before Elder Rasband focused his message on the positive influence bishops can have on individuals in their wards. Partway through his talk, he asked the congregation if anyone would stand and share an example of a bishop who had blessed their lives. Within a few seconds, a man stood up; someone brought him a microphone with a long cord so everyone could hear his story. Three or four other elders and high priests then took turns talking about bishops who had influenced them for good.

As they spoke, Jeff thought of the bishop who changed the course of his life by helping his family get sealed in the temple more than two decades earlier. He felt prompted to share the story but hesitated because no one in his stake knew that Jeff, who served in the Young Men presidency in his ward and had teenage quorum members in the audience, hadn't always been active in the Church. More than anything else, the current state of his marriage seemed too incongruent with the miracle of becoming an eternal family, so he remained in his seat.

The audience members who felt comfortable sharing their stories had all volunteered, and everyone waited quietly for the speaker to continue the rest of his talk. Instead, he said, "Brethren, I feel like there is one more story that needs to be told today." Then he waited for several moments of awkward silence. Finally, Jeff accepted the possibility that the speaker might be talking about him. He stood up, wondering if the initial prompting that morning had propelled him to this moment. Microphone in hand, he took a deep breath and launched into his story without even introducing himself. Whether Jeff forgot to say his name or felt too uncomfortable to announce it, he simply began in the middle.

"About twenty years ago, my wife and I were not going to church. We didn't get married in the temple and we had two energetic little boys, so it was just easier to stay home on Sundays. When we finally decided to try going back to church, we drove up to the student ward we had attended as newlyweds, even though we weren't students anymore. We had some friends in that ward and figured it would be easier to go where we knew someone.

"But when we got there, we found out that the schedule had changed and there wasn't a meeting at that time anymore. As we were wandering around the foyer, a bishop found us and introduced himself. He invited us into his office and talked to us for a while. He said we were welcome to attend that ward even though we weren't students.

"Over the next six months, that good brother helped us get completely reactivated with callings and temple recommends. And because of his help, we went and got sealed in the temple and had our two little boys sealed to us. This special bishop even offered to host a celebration party at his home, not knowing that we had ten siblings between the two of us and our extended family was almost 100 people." Tears streamed down Jeff's face as he concluded with, "I'm sure he doesn't even remember me, but our bishop at the time was Ronald Rasband!"

Immediately, Elder Rasband rose from his chair, pointed at him, and said firmly and loudly, "Jeff Matthews, I remember you."

After the meeting, Elder Rasband talked with Jeff and asked him to bring all his children to the 10:00 a.m. session of stake conference. Pulling together the sleepy teenagers and their married siblings took some serious convincing, but they managed to show up at the stake center. At the conclusion of that meeting, Elder Rasband sat down with Jeff's family in a classroom, where he met each one and encouraged them to stay strong in the gospel. He testified to them of God's love for each of them. Then, Elder Rasband asked for the current address of Jeff's wife so he could send a note of encouragement and support to her.

With conviction, he told Jeff, "You are going to be okay. Even if you can't save your marriage, you are going to be all right." His words sank deep into Jeff's heart and spread comfort through his soul.

When his wife returned to town and chose to get her own apartment, Jeff remembered Elder Rasband's assurance. And a year later, when he finally got divorced after almost three decades of marriage, the luminous stone he had picked up at stake conference helped him move forward with hope.

* * *

Jeff responded with meekness to a prompting to attend a 7:00 a.m. meeting that he could have easily skipped. In doing so, he received the balm that his soul needed. I admire those who have developed the ability to accept directions from the Spirit without arguing. I have questioned the seemingly illogical nature of several promptings, which seems unwise when I remember the outcome of looking at a brass serpent, washing seven times in the Jordan River, or blowing trumpets to defeat an enemy.[49] But even though the Lord has told us, "My thoughts are not your thoughts, neither are my ways your ways,"[50] I still sometimes resist revelation that doesn't make sense to my limited, mortal mind.

One evening, as I followed a recipe that yielded three loaves of artisan bread, the Spirit whispered to my mind, "Take one of those loaves to your aunt Laura." Thinking about how I would barely get dinner on the table in time for my hungry family, I balked at the idea of driving to my aunt's house during the busiest hour of my day. Showing up so close to dinner time also sounded useless. If I had gone an hour earlier, maybe, but by now, she had already made her own food. I completed this internal debate and got dinner on the table for my young kids. Again, the prompting came, this time even more specific and less logical. "Take her a loaf of bread first thing in the morning." Again, I argued, "The only reason I am even thinking about Laura is because this is *her* bread recipe!" I thought that showing up with day-old bread first thing in

---

49. Numbers 21:8; 2 Kings 5:10-13; Joshua 6:4-5.
50. Isaiah 55:8.

the morning would seem like an afterthought. It wouldn't be hot; it wouldn't be fresh. How unimpressive. I stubbornly concluded that I would not deliver bread to Laura in the morning.

The next day, my mom called to tell me that my aunt Laura's mother had been out walking early that morning when a car hit and killed her. My heart dropped as I realized how I could have been on Laura's porch with a loaf of homemade bread as a messenger of God's love. I could almost hear the Lord saying, "As the heavens are higher than the earth, so are my ways higher than your ways, and my thoughts than your thoughts."[51] I could have been on His errand! I could have stood at her door in her dark hour and said, "I don't know why, but I've been thinking about you and the Holy Ghost told me to come." And she would have known that God was aware of her. I prayed through my tears of regret that someone with a soul less "rebellious and proud as mine"[52] had followed a similar prompting. I know from my experience with Ruth at book club that some disciples have learned not to argue with the Spirit, thereby becoming what Elder Holland described when he said, "Not all angels are from the other side of the veil. Some of them reside in our own neighborhoods."[53]

Remember, spiritual experiences often appear as straightforward, ordinary events on the surface. An outside observer without the Holy Ghost would probably not consider some moments worth recording. But I learned to listen to the Spirit because of things like dirty jeans and day-old bread. I want my children to have these simple stories because they shaped my testimony in powerful ways.

* * *

Luckily, I learned from my missed opportunity to be "on the Lord's errand,"[54] and tried to improve my response time—and attitude.

---

51. Isaiah 55:9.
52. Charles H. Gabriel, "I Stand All Amazed," *Hymns of The Church of Jesus Christ of Latter-day Saints* (Salt Lake City: The Church of Jesus Christ of Latter-day Saints, 1985).
53. Jeffrey R. Holland, "The Ministry of Angels" *Ensign*, November 2008.
54. Thomas S. Monson, "The Sacred Call of Service" *Ensign*, May 2005.

Another strong prompting came in a slightly surprising place. While receiving revelation in the temple doesn't sound unusual, the way this message arrived caught me off guard. I sat in a quiet chapel and felt peace but did not get instructions. I made covenants in the endowment room and felt happy but did not receive any promptings. Finally, I meditated and prayed in the celestial room, where I felt connected to heaven but not assigned to take specific action. For whatever reason, a stall in the locker room became the most holy spot for me that day. In the middle of changing my clothes, a clear prompting sliced through my thoughts. "Give your temple apron[55] to Jessie."

I couldn't believe it. My shock stemmed from three distinct reasons. First, I recognized immediately that the thought hadn't occurred as a first-person idea. I didn't have the words, "*I* should give *my* temple apron to Jessie," suddenly appear in my consciousness. Second, I would never come up with such a distasteful task for myself, as I absolutely treasured my handmade temple apron. My Grandma Janet gave it to me after her mother died, and I felt honored to wear a piece of temple clothing that had belonged to my great-grandmother. So, I had no doubt about whether the command originated in my own mind, both because of the wording and the nature of the task. Finally, I knew that my sister did not currently own a temple recommend and showed no interest in getting one. Would I really have to hand over a treasured keepsake to someone who would neither appreciate nor use it?

But not only did I resolve to carry out this task, I also knew without a doubt that Grandma Janet wanted me to do it. I felt like she was standing right next to me in the temple, telling me to give her gift to my sister. The next weekend, I wrapped my beloved apron in white tissue paper, placed it in a sack, and drove up the canyon. I knew that the loss of the apron would have no impact on my ability to worship or feel the Spirit, but I still felt a twinge of sadness. However, a new emotion crept into my heart; the closer I got to Jessie's house, the more nervous I felt. Talking about the temple sounded awkward. What if she got uncomfortable? What if she didn't believe my story or rejected my gift? I also worried about offending my beautiful younger sister,

---

55. "Sacred Temple Clothing," https://www.churchofjesuschrist.org/temples/sacred-temple-clothing?lang=eng.

who had traveled a far rockier road than I had. I certainly didn't want her to view this encounter as a lecture.

We sat on the back patio, just the two of us. She could tell that I felt nervous and ordered, "Just say it!" So, I told the truth.

"I was in the temple, and I felt strongly that Grandma Janet wanted me to give you my temple apron." I handed it to her, and she replied with a casual, even tone.

"I'm not going to use it."

"I know. But I have to give it to you. I was hoping we could just trade."

She stood up and went to get her temple apron from her closet. When she came back, she said, "Mine is just a standard issue," and handed it to me. I tried not to mentally compare the color, stitching, and sentimental value of the exchanged items.

"Thank you."

I breathed a sigh of relief, then caught my breath again when she said, "You know, you're not the first person in our family to deliver a message to me from Grandma Janet." She didn't elaborate, and my respect for other people's sacred experiences slightly outweighed my intense curiosity. Many months went by before I heard other pieces of the story. Eventually, I learned that in another temple on a different day, our mom had a clear impression that Grandma Janet, her mother, wanted to communicate to her the idea that "if Jessic comes back to the temple, she will have a happy life."

When my mom and I told Jessie about our individual experiences, we had no idea that my sister Sadie had already sent Jessie an email detailing a series of sacred moments that occurred in a temple hundreds of miles away. Since God uses a variety of ways to communicate with us, in contrast to the words in my mind, Sadie received personal revelation in the form of images. At the beginning of an endowment session, she felt the Spirit very strongly and at that exact moment sensed the presence of Grandma Janet. She saw her face clearly and suddenly in her mind. Then, as Sadie looked down at her hands, she "saw" Grandma Janet's hands alongside her own. Elder Dieter F. Uchtdorf taught, "There are more ways to see than with our eyes,"[56] and Sadie testified of this in her email to Jessie:

---

56. Dieter F. Uchtdorf, "Fourth Floor, Last Door" *Ensign*, November 2016.

> I don't know how that all works exactly, but I know she was with me. It seemed as if she was witnessing to me the truthfulness of what I was watching, hearing, and feeling. I've never had a spiritual experience remotely close to this one. All I know is it was real. It happened. Grandma was in that temple that night and I "saw" her with me.
>
> But that's not all. After the first few times I experienced this, you popped into my mind. I hadn't been thinking about you or praying for you. But the next few times I "saw" Grandma, thoughts of you simultaneously filled my mind. I felt strongly that if you made it back to the temple, you would have a similar experience. You would feel the love of God and of Grandma.

Three witnesses testified to Jessie that someone on the other side of the veil cared about her spiritual well-being. A year and a half later, Jessie not only had a temple recommend, but she also woke up at 3:00 a.m. every Wednesday to serve in the temple as an ordinance worker. Somehow, she balanced working full-time as a nurse, serving as the Primary president in her ward, and showing up for her temple shift every week. If she sometimes felt stretched thin, compensatory blessings gave her enough energy to connect with her Primary kids and even buy a set of scriptures for a little boy who came to Primary although his family were not members of the Church.

When the Salt Lake temple closed for renovations, Jessie worked as a shift coordinator at the Jordan River temple, located even farther away from her home. Blessed with an ability to sense the joy of her brothers and sisters in the spirit world, Jessie told us that when she helps people perform ordinances, she knows that their ancestors are "having a party in heaven!" I'm sure that when Grandma Janet saw Jessie return to the house of the Lord, she had a party of her own.

* * *

I have a strong testimony of the reality of the spirit world. Several luminous stones along my path have convinced me that spirits on the other side of the veil want to help us and want us to help them. When my husband, Jeff, lost his eighty-two-year-old mother to breast cancer, he asked me if I wanted to go with him to the mortuary to plan her funeral. Since he has seven siblings, I knew they had plenty of possibilities for speakers, along with an abundance of opinions. I expressed my willingness to attend as emotional support, but we agreed that it made more sense for me to take care of things at home. I felt a little bit relieved, in part because I had only joined the family three years earlier, while many of the other in-laws had been around for decades. I felt comfortable with my plan to simply attend the funeral and did not expect to help plan or participate in the program.

However, something strange happened the morning that Jeff met with his siblings. I took my car to get the oil changed, and just as I pulled out of the parking lot, before I could turn on any music that might have distracted me, a clear thought came to my mind. "You should arrange a musical number for Jeff's mom's funeral." I immediately launched an argument against that idea, since I have no musical background, training, or talent. I added to my internal debate that I had the least amount of influence in the imaginary family hierarchy. Self-conscious and unsure of my role as the new wife of the oldest brother, I felt that I didn't have any right to alter this important event.

Ten minutes later, the thought came to me again, this time with more detail. "You should see if Marshall McDonald can come and play the piano at Jeff's mom's funeral." Marshall, a talented pianist and composer, arranges sacred music for numerous well-known artists. He and I spent all three years of high school as close friends but had not stayed in touch after he got married. The unusual specifics of this prompting opened more opportunities for me to push back. I argued with myself, "I haven't talked to Marshall for twenty years! I can't call him up now and ask him for a favor. I don't even have his phone number."

I tried to forget about it, but I could not shake the prompting. Finally, I softened my heart enough to pay attention to what the Spirit told me. Simultaneously, the possibility began to grow into an idea that made my heart rate increase. In recent years, Marshall had arranged several "mash-ups," combining two melodies of well-known songs that didn't initially seem to belong together. I started to wonder how amazing it would be if Marshall came to Jeff's mom's funeral and played an instrumental version of her favorite song, "Happy," by Pharrell Williams. I imagined a scene where her kids and grandkids were listening to a hymn or a Primary song and then suddenly began to recognize the melody of her anthem. Picturing it brought tears to my eyes, and I decided that I had to at least try to accomplish what the Spirit directed me to do.

I looked up my old friend on social media and sent a private message through an app that I rarely used. Feeling slightly pessimistic, I reminded myself that I have read messages in that app several *weeks* after friends sent them because I don't check it every day. I had no idea if Marshall would even read the message before the upcoming funeral.

A mere twenty minutes later, I had a reply. He said that he was rarely on social media "but just happened to see" my message. That was the first tender mercy. The second came in the next sentence as he told me of his willingness to play at the funeral! Finally, a third miracle occurred. His schedule lined up perfectly because he doesn't teach institute classes on Monday mornings, the day Jeff's siblings had selected to celebrate the life of their mom. I sat in shock at how the pieces fell into place.

The next hurdle proved more difficult. I had to convince Jeff and his many siblings of the idea. I went to Jeff with my thrilling story about my prompting and how Marshall responded. Jeff's response deflated my enthusiasm as he expressed appreciation that I investigated the possibility but explained that they already worried about the length of the program. Every sibling wanted to speak and had committed to keeping the program under an hour, which left six minutes for each person to share their favorite memories. The group had already cut out verses from the opening and closing hymn to try to save time. Jeff concluded by reminding me that his mom wanted the grandchildren to sing, and his siblings would never agree to another musical number.

I could tell that there was no way to get Marshall in the program unless I shared the secret with Jeff. I had really wanted to surprise him with the actual song, so I felt conflicted, but I recognized it as my only shot. After I explained how Marshall could incorporate "Happy" into a traditional hymn, Jeff didn't hesitate. "We have to make that happen.

I will talk to Tim." Tim had been assigned to print the programs, and Jeff decided that he and Tim could add it to the program without telling the other siblings. He explained to him why we wanted to do it, and Tim agreed to list a special musical number without disclosing the song.

I sent Marshall a few video clips of Jeff's mom dancing to "Happy." We have footage of her leading the entire family in a dance party to that song at our family reunion and a few seconds of her jamming out to it at a granddaughter's wedding reception. One of her daughters even helped her make a music video where she lip-synced to the entire song while doing various activities in multiple locations. I wanted Marshall to get a sense for her vibrant personality and how much the song meant to her.

Marshall understood my request and assured me that he could blend the pop song into a sacred hymn in a way that would not detract from the spirit of the meeting. He even cited another similar mash-up he had arranged that included "Come, Come, Ye Saints" and "Let it Be," by the Beatles. Then, he asked me, "Does the family want to choose the hymn that would be the prominent song in the arrangement, or should I choose that?" I checked with Jeff and Tim, but none of the suggestions that we talked about felt quite right. I knew that I wanted it to be something familiar to the grandchildren so they would listen and hear the surprise. If the first few bars of the melody didn't catch their attention, they might miss the important moment that we hoped to create.

Texting back and forth, Jeff and Marshall and I brainstormed, but I continued to feel unsatisfied. We wanted the song to focus on the Savior, but many of the appropriate hymns would not engage the kids. The grandchildren planned to sing two Primary songs, so we couldn't use either of those familiar tunes. Determined to find the perfect vehicle for our surprise, I prayed for help in selecting a hymn that would somehow fit all our criteria by catching the attention of the younger family members, maintaining the spirit of the funeral, blending with an upbeat pop song, and honoring a resilient and relentlessly positive woman. With all of those goals in mind, it seemed wrong to pick a song at random.

One night, Jeff and I sat at the dining room table, looking for pictures to include in the slide show the family planned to display at the viewing. After I finished gathering digital photos from a family vacation, several reunions, and a birthday dinner, the thought came to me to look in my text thread with Jeff's mom for other pictures. I could not imagine what other picture I might have shared with her that I had not already carefully selected from the chronological photos. But, in a conscious effort to be more receptive to promptings, I resisted my habit of arguing with ideas that come into my head like that. Jeff's mom and I hadn't exchanged many texts, so it didn't take long to scroll through the messages. After a few seconds, my eyes rested on this brief conversation from July 2017, two years earlier:

> ME: Good morning! Do you have two songs that you would like Jeff to add to the playlist for our road trip? We will all try to guess who submitted which song. :)
>
> JAN MATTHEWS: "Happy" and "I'm Trying to Be Like Jesus."

When I saw that, I couldn't believe it. I felt like she was standing in my dining room, whispering to me. I turned my phone to show the screen to Jeff and said, "This is the other song that she wants." I sent a screenshot to Marshall to let him know our search for the perfect song was over.

I can't imagine a more fitting tribute than Marshall's personalized arrangement. The message of those intertwined songs summed up her life: "I'm Trying to Be Like Jesus," and that is why I'm "Happy." As the unexpected melody emerged—undoubtably for the first time in an LDS chapel—I caught Jeff's eye as he sat on the stand. I felt that the Spirit had enabled me to offer comfort and honor Jeff's mom in a unique way that meant something to him. That alone would have been enough, though many family members experienced profound peace and comfort as Marshall played the piano. For many weeks, I marveled at the simple, quiet ways the Holy Ghost had guided the entire process.

* * *

It seems clear that our Heavenly Parents don't want us to stay in our comfort zones all the time. They might even relish giving us opportunities to have conversations or do things that make us feel uncomfortable, nervous, or out of our league. We can only grow if we stretch. And the more we allow God to prevail in our lives,[57] the more He can bless us.

When my parents had a young family, my dad worked as an attorney during the day and remodeled our house at night. Those time-consuming responsibilities, along with a church calling and four kids, kept him so busy that he didn't get many hours of sleep. Always running on empty, if he tried to just sit and listen to the speakers in sacrament meeting, he ended up nodding off before the closing hymn. So, to keep himself awake, he quietly sketched on graph paper during the meeting. My dad spent an hour every Sunday for years drawing floor plans for a dream house he hoped to build someday. He kept the sketches in a manila folder in a file drawer in his office. I watched his collection of floor plans grow until the time came to turn the dream into a reality.

My youngest sibling had graduated from high school and had received a mission call. The rest of us had gotten married, and my parents no longer felt the need to live in the neighborhood where they had deliberately stayed to not uproot us from our schools and friends. Now, they began the "empty nester" chapter of their lives by acquiring some land in the mountains and starting their dream house. In addition to a law degree, my dad had a general contractor license, so he spent every spare hour at the construction site. He drew the plans to get the building permits. He drove the backhoe to dig the hole for the foundation. He ordered materials and oversaw every step of the process. Though he hired specialty crews for certain aspects of the construction, my dad did all the work he possibly could, including dry wall, paint, and electrical work. This process took an entire year. Later, my mom would subtract that year when someone asked her how long they had been married, explaining how she saw so little of him that it didn't count.

---

57. Russell M. Nelson, "Let God Prevail," *Ensign*, November 2020.

As soon as the house had finished walls, my mom got more involved, selecting tile, hardwood floors, and cabinets. She evaluated dozens of fixtures, measured furniture, and ran errands to check the color of carpet, drapes, and countertops. Together, my dad and mom created the home they had talked about for years. They worked relentlessly to get the details exactly right. My dad measured and cut the baseboards and molding. In the upstairs game room, they installed the thickest carpet pad they could find, followed by soft, spongy carpet so their young adult kids could lounge on the floor and talk for hours. The great room downstairs had a rock fireplace, vaulted ceilings, and deep, luxurious couches facing huge windows that framed the yellow quaking aspen on the side of Quarry Mountain.

When they finished their dream house, the people who loved them rejoiced at the gorgeous result of their all-consuming, long-term project. For twenty years, they had worked to get to a place financially where they could build a house like this. Everyone who had followed the story, from my proud grandparents to the technical writers in the cubicles next to me at work, celebrated my parents' dream home, the house in which they planned to live for the rest of their lives.

We only celebrated one Christmas in that house. One morning, my dad woke up with the strongest impression that they needed to sell the house they had built from scratch with their talents, skills, ideas, time, and sweat. He told my mom, "I think that the Holy Ghost is prompting me that we need to sell our house." Despite her shock, she immediately agreed to follow the guidance he had received from the Lord. The rest of us could not believe this was happening. How on earth could they give up this house? They could not buy another one like it for any amount of money; a second home specifically designed around their personalities and passions did not exist.

My dad simply said that they had accrued considerable debt in the process and now felt that the Lord wanted them to get out of debt by selling their home and buying an existing house somewhere else. They obediently and prayerfully drove around through nearby areas in the middle of the winter on muddy, unpaved roads. When they found a house that they felt prompted to purchase, they made an offer on it even though they hadn't sold their dream house yet. Owning two houses brought additional stress and uncertainty, but they proceeded with faith that the Lord wanted them to move forward.

Soon, an ecstatic buyer agreed to pay for the serene, spacious Quarry Mountain house. My siblings and I grieved the loss of the great room and the porch swing but grieved the loss of the dream-turned-reality even more. We had loved watching my dad's excitement at every stage of the building process as he created that home. We couldn't understand why they had to give it up and absolutely marveled at how my parents didn't seem resentful or frustrated about it. My mom only mentioned how she would miss all the wildlife that she saw on her daily hikes and from the windows of their beautiful house, since the hillside started right outside their back door.

Thankfully, many small tender mercies confirmed their impression about the new house. A large bookcase that they had designed for the Quarry Mountain home fit in the new family room with a mere half inch on either side. A wall that had an unused supporting vertical post for no apparent reason made it possible to add a much-needed mud room. Soon, my mom received a call to serve as the Relief Society president in a ward that could genuinely appreciate her quirky, down-to-earth personality, and when she arrived at the enrichment service activity in a ponytail and her Tina Turner concert T-shirt, she felt loved and accepted. A large covered porch became the perfect place to watch hummingbirds, and they discovered that a moose lived in their front yard.

To the rest of us, it seemed that they simply found the silver linings they sought and surely deserved. But then, news reports revealed the most significant, underlying blessing of all, one that would benefit my parents for years to come. The housing market crashed. Overnight, the Quarry Mountain house dramatically dropped in perceived value. If they had remained in their dream home, they likely could not have afforded to live there because of the real estate market and the economy, but they also would never have been able to sell it at the price they did. Another owner in the same development actively tried to sell the house down the street for six years without success. We had no way to know at the time what an emotional and financial burden that house would have become, but God knew, and my parents allowed His will to prevail in their lives.

* * *

Sometimes, we get to hear the happy ending of a story, but experiences with promptings don't always include crescendos or tidy conclusions. One of my favorite examples of this had the "outward appearance" of an ordinary event. When my brother James served his mission in Ukraine, he had a companion with whom he didn't talk much. But although they didn't enjoy extra conversations or immediately connect as friends, they worked diligently to share the gospel.

One evening, as they silently walked home from a teaching appointment, James had a "weird, bad, and scary feeling" come over him. Just then, his companion said, "I have a weird feeling about being here. Something doesn't feel right." They decided to cross the street at once. When they had reached the other side, they both felt the concern lifted from them. As a sense of calm spread through his body, James thought, "Okay. We are okay now."

Guess what happened next? Nothing. They did not see a car run off the road right where they would have been standing, they did not later hear about a crime committed in a nearby alley, and they did not meet an eager investigator on their way home. To anyone watching, nothing remarkable occurred. Two young men crossed the road to get to the other side . . . and there was no punch line.

Yet, twenty years later, James cannot tell this story without tears in his eyes because in that moment, he knew he had received a warning from God through the Holy Ghost. Having two witnesses who independently recognized an identical prompting has made it impossible for James to compartmentalize or rationalize that moment. And because he recorded it in his journal, he remembers it clearly and will treasure it as a luminous stone for the rest of his life.

I am confident that you have followed a prompting from the Holy Ghost, to call someone, go somewhere, or let go of something that weighed you down. It does not need to sound thrilling or take more than a paragraph to explain. The next few pages provide space for you to respond to the starters in this chapter. Additional blank pages follow for other moments you are ready to record.

When have you been an instrument in the hands of the Lord to answer someone else's prayer?

Have you ever acted on a prompting to talk to someone whom you would not have approached on your own? What happened?

When have you received direction from the Spirit that you knew was not from your own mind because it was something that you didn't want to do?

Has the Holy Ghost ever delivered a message to you of correction or chastisement or showed you an area of weakness to help you repent?

Have you ever followed a warning from the Holy Ghost hat protected you from potential danger? What was the outcome?

CHAPTER 6
Building Faith

By writing personal and family histories, we are helped immeasurably in gaining a true, eternal perspective of life. Writing our histories with the proper blend of fact and feeling (and so often, feelings in spiritual things are the real facts) gives us a deep spiritual insight into the meaning and purpose of our lives.[58]

—Elder John H. Groberg

During my early childhood, I only knew about one role of the Holy Ghost: to comfort us. Precept upon precept, my understanding grew, and I came to learn that the Holy Ghost can also guide and warn us. When that constituted my entire view of the Spirit, I valued His companionship immensely, so you can imagine how my gratitude soared when I learned that He also testifies of truth. I remember finding out that we cannot have a testimony of God and Jesus Christ without the Holy Ghost. Sometimes, spiritual experiences don't involve an answer to prayer or a prompting to act but simply build our faith as the Spirit illuminates our minds.

---

58. John H. Groberg, "Writing Your Personal and Family History" *Ensign*, May 1980.

Cal Brown, a young newlywed in our ward, gave a refreshingly honest talk in sacrament meeting. He spoke of the frustration he felt on his mission when he didn't have the life-changing experiences he thought he would. Before embarking on his own proselyting adventure, he had heard many return missionaries tell inspiring stories in their homecoming talks. Cal wanted to see exciting changes in people's lives and have interactions with investigators that he could tell people about when he got home.

For months, he continued to study the scriptures and pray for miracles, but nothing surprising or dramatic happened to him. He testified, "I learned that there are no life-changing experiences. There are only life-changing choices." Using Laman and Lemuel as examples, he talked about how some people experience dramatic moments but are not changed by them. We read in 1 Nephi that "after the angel had departed, Laman and Lemuel again began to murmur."[59] They had an outward miracle, but not an inward change of heart. In contrast, Cal didn't witness any amazing events but instead had a gradual increase of light[60] as his scripture study strengthened his faith in Jesus Christ over the course of his mission. President Nelson has promised us that we can "*receive more* faith by doing something that *requires more* faith."[61] Cal followed that counsel when he continued to study the word of God daily even though he didn't see miracles.

Over the years, I've attended dozens of mission homecomings, including those of my high school friends, handfuls of cousins, and youth in my ward. Subsequently, I have heard many uplifting stories of "golden investigators" and conversion miracles. Some brought tears to my eyes when I heard them because the Spirit witnessed the truth of what the missionary said. I'm sure those sacred stories built the testimonies of many people. But right now, I can't remember any of them. I wonder if Cal would have guessed that his story about nothing exciting happening on his mission would stick in my mind longer than any of the dramatic stories he once envied. I return to his

---

59. 1 Nephi 3:31.
60. David A. Bednar, "The Spirit of Revelation" *Ensign*, May 2011.
61. Russell M. Nelson, "Christ Is Risen; Faith in Him Will Move Mountains" *Liahona*, May 2021.

example again and again as I consider the impact and accumulation of my small, life-changing choices.

Moving through our day-to-day routines, we have hundreds of opportunities to choose to believe in Jesus Christ and follow Him in intentional ways. If you have experienced a gradual increase of faith in Jesus Christ and can't think of a notable event or experience that built your testimony, the following starter questions might help spark a memory.

Starters

- Which of God's creations has helped you feel the Spirit or increased your faith?
- Have you had any experiences that increased your testimony of a particular principle of the gospel or the blessings of keeping a specific commandment?
- Have you ever joined other people in praying and fasting for a common purpose? How did you feel about it?
- Did a trial or difficult circumstances in your life ever build your faith in God?
- Have you ever felt your testimony grow when you shared the gospel with someone else?

Stories

After my divorce, my sister Jessie invited me on a road trip to southern Utah. I usually spent every other weekend with my kids and every other weekend missing them terribly, so I knew it would help me to have a change of scenery. Laughing with Jessie as we hiked in Bryce Canyon proved good medicine for my mind, body, and spirit.

I hadn't prayed for any specific answers, but the Lord knew of my heartache and provided personal revelation that strengthened my faith. As we hiked through delicate rock columns and formations called "hoodoos," the Spirit whispered to my mind. As a young child, I had learned that wind and water form hoodoos through erosion; now, as I looked at them through the lens of my recent suffering, the thought came to me that the red rock hoodoos are beautiful because of what they have lost. They are unique, amazing shapes because of what has been taken away.

As I was pondering this personal revelation, another clear thought entered my mind: "What is left is the strongest part." In that moment, my belief in the reality of God deepened as I felt connected to Him through His creations.

* * *

Trials shape us like wind and water carve sandstone, revealing our strength over time. Soft spoken but consistently displaying a wry sense of humor, my brother-in-law, Matt, became a hoodoo of quiet fortitude as he fought cancer. For years, his witty side comments put people at ease, made them feel included, and left us all laughing appreciatively. He never said anything unkind, and he showed an abundance of love and patience to his teenage son, who has Down syndrome.

When Matt received a diagnosis of stage 4 Non-Hodgkin's Lymphoma, my husband and I joined a handful of people who shaved their heads in support. Matt's year-long treatment plan included several rounds of chemotherapy and a stem cell transplant. Unfortunately, after he finished his third round of chemotherapy and went in for an evaluation, the doctors said that his scan showed too much metabolic activity, meaning that the tumor was not in good enough remission to start the transplant process. Matt and his wife, JaNae, decided to go to a different hospital, where Matt did a fourth round of chemo. Then, he developed an infection, and his body again wasn't ready for the stem cell collection. The doctors explained that if they waited too long, the tumor would become active again and require additional cycles of chemotherapy, which would again weaken Matt's immune system, perpetuating a vicious cycle. Every day, Matt went to the hospital to check his white blood cell count. The doctors said that when the number rose to a certain target level, Matt could receive a shot of a medication to allow collection of his stem cells.

When we heard about the situation, Jeff and I wanted to do something to help. We decided to fast for Matt and ask others to join us. Feeling that this constituted an emergency, I wanted Matt to have the strongest people praying for him, even if they didn't know him personally. I thought about the faith of my stake patriarch, my grandfather, and my former college roommate. I couldn't help but think of other friends who have a close relationship with our Father in Heaven, people who pray with sincere, fervent intent. I sent text messages to a few former coworkers, two ladies in my ward, and my aunt Kay, giving them details so they could make their prayers specific. They all responded by text to say that they would pray for Matt, which filled my heart with gratitude for wonderful people in my life who have demonstrated great faith.

Then, I thought of our friends in Kenya and considered how powerful it would be to have people all over the world praying for Matt. In an hour and a half, I had sent messages to thirty-three people in six countries, explaining exactly what Matt needed. The next time I prayed, out loud and on my knees, I could feel the prayers of others as the Spirit connected us.

When our kids came home from school, I told them how dire the situation was. We hadn't done our monthly fast Sunday yet because we fast together as a family on the first Sunday of the month when the kids wake up at our house, not always on the actual first Sunday of the month. That way, we can fast together without it negatively impacting the time that they spend with their dad. He loves to cook breakfast on Sunday mornings, and we don't want to take away from that tradition.

I invited the kids to fast for Matt, and I told them that our plan was to fast for dinner. They immediately expressed concerns about that, since they have only ever fasted breakfast or breakfast and lunch. I told them that they could have an after school snack at 4:00 but that we wouldn't eat dinner or bedtime snacks. They had never gone to bed hungry but agreed to try. I let them eat substantial after school snacks at 4:00 p.m., but I knew that they wouldn't eat again until morning, a difficult situation for kids who eat as frequently as mine do. Homework only distracted them for an hour, and a little after our normal dinner time, Kate started to get hungry and talk about food. By 9:00 p.m., Bear was lying on the floor in the kitchen, saying that he really, really needed to eat something before he went to bed. He agreed that he would survive without food but insisted that he needed to drink some water. I encouraged him to stick with it and expressed my confidence that he could do this. I asked him, "Tomorrow, when we get good news, don't you want to know that you were part of the miracle?"

He answered, "How do you know we're going to get good news?"

That question hit me hard as I realized I would have to put my faith on the line. I had to consider what I really believed and what it would mean if the news came back negative. Would that mean that Heavenly Father recognized our fasting and prayers but had a better plan for Matt and JaNae's family? I truly do believe that all things work together for the good of those that put their trust in the Lord.[62]

I replied, "It will be good news. Do you know why? Do you know what I have prayed for? When I prayed today on my knees out loud, fasting all day long, I didn't just ask Heavenly Father to bless Matt so that his numbers would go up. I prayed that his white blood cell count would go up so much that the doctors would be surprised. And that the nurses and doctors would ask Matt and JaNae what they had done to change those levels so much and they would be able to testify that it was because of the power of prayer."

Bear didn't whine anymore after that, and he didn't drink any water before bed. When I tucked him in, he asked me, "If I don't fall asleep, will you let me eat or drink something?" I assured him that we would let him have a sip of water if he was unable to fall asleep but that I thought he would fall asleep quickly. And he did.

I got down on my knees in my bedroom and prayed with great focus and energy. I told Heavenly Father that in addition to a miracle for Matt, I now also needed a miracle for my kids. Begging Him to grant us this blessing, I explained (although I knew that He already understood) that a faith-building experience would add oil to their lamps[63] and strengthen them against the negative ideas and opinions about religion that they will encounter. I felt the Spirit as I prayed. I felt like I had set my soul to a frequency that hummed in the electrified air above me, just for a moment.

The next morning, Jeff went out early and got everyone's favorite bagels—cinnamon sugar and asiago cheese. Everyone left for school and work with full stomachs and hopeful hearts, anxious for the news that they hoped we would have by the time they got home from school. I went to the temple, where I prayed in the celestial room after completing an endowment session.

---

62. Romans 8:28.
63. Matthew 25:1–13.

When I came out of the temple, I couldn't even wait until I got in my car to check for text messages from Jeff, so I sat on the bench next to the wall of the temple with the carved words, "Holiness to the Lord, House of the Lord." I looked at my phone and saw a message in which Jeff had copied and pasted a text from JaNae:

> Ok latest update. His white cell count jumped from 2.8 to 7. That is significant. The nurse even asked what had happened to cause 'such a jump.' We told her lots of people are praying/fasting for him. He also was able to sleep in a bit this morning so that was good. So, they were able to test the cd34 stem cell count and we should hear back from them by tonight. If they are high enough, then he could start collection tomorrow!! Thanks so much.

Absolutely overwhelmed with the love of God, I sat stunned. I pride myself on my optimism and I've developed a solid belief in the power of prayer, so I did expect the numbers to go up. But I couldn't believe that not only had the nurse reacted the way I prayed that a medical professional would, but JaNae also took the time to include that detail in her update. And there I had it on my phone to read to my kids! I felt humbled by the abundant goodness of our Father in Heaven. What a personal gift.

That evening, when Jeff picked up Bear from lacrosse practice, he asked if Bear had heard the latest news. Then he read JaNae's text out loud, and Bear responded, "It happened just the way my mom said it would." When they got home, we all sat in the family room and talked about the numbers. The increase in Matt's white blood cells enabled the doctors to administer a drug to improve his CD34 count, the number that indicates whether someone has the right amount of hematopoietic stem cells for a successful transplantation. That number needed to hit 10 to start the stem cell collection.

We kept praying for Matt. Five days later, they found out that his CD34 count had gone from .9 to 35, and they collected the stem cells for the transplant that ultimately saved his life. I sent texts to everyone who had prayed for Matt, thanking them for their part in the miracle.

I'm sure iconoclasts would argue that with the medication, the numbers would have gone up even without the prayers and the fasting. But the white blood cell count improved significantly even before they administered the medication. In addition, the power of prayer may have enabled Matt's body to respond to the medicine in a positive way. Many times, cancer patients suffer from reactions or adverse side effects that force caregivers to try to find a different treatment.

Elder L. Whitney Clayton taught:

> The decision to believe is the most important choice we ever make. It shapes all our other decisions. . . . Belief and testimony and faith . . . do not just happen to us. Belief is something we choose . . . we work for it, and we sacrifice for it. We will not accidentally come to believe in the Savior and His gospel any more than we will accidentally pray or pay tithing. We actively choose to believe, just like we choose to keep other commandments.[64]

In this case, I choose to believe that the medication and the prayers worked together to provide a miracle. The experience brought our family closer together and filled me with gratitude for my network of righteous friends. Moreover, it built my faith in Jesus Christ and increased the faith of my kids.

* * *

I feel grateful for Primary teachers who helped me create an association between the Holy Ghost and the phrase, "still, small voice."[65] This description reminds us that most of our moments of revelation would not make a good movie. The exciting experience with Matt's blood count built our faith but hundreds of tiny, quiet experiences have added more to my testimony than any startling event.

---

64. L. Whitney Clayton, "Choose to Believe" *Ensign*, May 2015.
65. 1 Kings 19:11–12.

Most of the sacred experiences that bless my life and nourish my spirit occur in the middle of ordinary and even mundane routines. Subtle and short, those whisperings of the Spirit disappear if we don't identify and act on them. Often, our choice to do something ultimately proves to us that the idea came from the Holy Ghost. I am thankful for the miracles that appear in the middle of everyday tasks.

I procrastinate several household chores on a regular basis but none with as much deliberate avoidance as sorting through the dozens of pieces of paper that come into our house. These papers almost seem to have magnetic properties. Instead of finding their way into the garbage, they attract each other, pulling themselves into inefficient piles of flyers, worksheets, lists, mail, notes, and handouts. The piles grow on the counter, on the bench in my bedroom, and on the ledge in the stairwell, becoming more daunting to sift and sort. Every few weeks, I sit down and organize the papers, deciding if each one prompts an action or requires recycling.

After the Christmas season ends each year, we have several family birthdays in January, creating the perfect motivation to clean the house so we can host our kids and grandkids. A weekend of vigorous cleaning once granted me a Monday morning where I found myself without any straightening, vacuuming, dusting, or scrubbing to do. That meant that the piles of paper had finally reached the top of the task list, after quietly growing taller since before the holidays started. I began to gather and sort papers from church, including notes from my Sunday School lessons, programs from sacrament meetings, pictures the kids drew as they (hopefully) listened to talks, and so on. I carefully identified the papers that I wanted to save. Suddenly, I remembered that I had never typed up the priesthood blessings that Jeff gave the kids the night before the first day of school. How could I have forgotten to do that? We were already halfway through the school year. I promised myself that I would prioritize that important-but-not-urgent task that I had neglected.

I woke up the next morning before any of the kids and transcribed the three priesthood blessings from audio files on my phone. As I typed the words and read them out loud to make sure I hadn't missed anything, my heart started beating faster as I realized how the blessings had been fulfilled over the prior five months. Reading them with an entire semester of hindsight, the promises from the Lord connected with actual events that I had witnessed. Later, I told Jeff about my experience, adding, "I'm sure it would be easy for someone to claim that the same things would have happened even if they had not gotten these blessings."

I paused, trying to remember the wording of the verse in the Doctrine and Covenants 59:21, but before I could quote it, Jeff said, "But we are supposed to confess God's hand in all things." I smiled at one of the "meant-to-be" moments that strengthen us through the ups and downs of blended family life.

Priesthood blessings have become a gauge of sorts for our stepfamily, allowing us to measure our slow but steady progress. During the first year of our marriage, the new school year blessings brought tears and heartache when Jeff automatically referred to them as "father's blessings," causing awkward feelings for my kids, who adore their dad. We all felt a painful juxtaposition of the phrase "father's blessings" and the knowledge that their own father had left the Church.

A year later, we didn't even attempt to offer the kids any priesthood blessings from Jeff because he—and they—were all still recovering from the previous experience. The third year, they each got a blessing, and it went smoothly. The fourth year, he gave them each a blessing and our teenage daughter, Kate, immediately conveyed her appreciation with an enthusiastic and sincere, "Thank you! That was a very thoughtful blessing." That meant the world to her sweet stepdad. So, this recurring event indicates some healing and bonding, answers to countless prayers.

I must admit, I had never reread any of the school year blessings that I carefully record and type for the kids to save. Transcribing blessings has always brought the Spirit into my heart, but reading them months later deepened my faith in the power of priesthood blessings in a new way. As I studied them, the Holy Ghost testified to me that the blessings had indeed impacted the way certain events unfolded for Kate, Bear, and Scout.

Kate's blessing included a promise that she would become more comfortable with learning to drive a car. In August, when Jeff gave her this blessing, Kate felt enormous amounts of anxiety about learning to drive. The most convenient and natural time for her to get comfortable behind the wheel of a car would have been over the summer since she had a flexible schedule with many free hours. We knew it made sense to do the forty hours of supervised driving during the summer, but she panicked every time I mentioned it. It wasn't until months later that she gained more confidence and finally enjoyed learning to drive. I believe that the priesthood blessing that Jeff gave her helped her with this.

He also blessed her to be able to balance her workload at school with possible opportunities to travel. We weren't sure in August whether Kate would have the chance to travel to Kenya on a humanitarian trip. But after the school year started, her spot on the trip became a reality. Then, we discovered a wonderful tender mercy: the Kenya trip happened to coincide with the end of the first quarter. So, instead of having to miss eight days of school in a single term, Kate missed two days of the first quarter, a couple of days of fall break, and four days of the next quarter. That made it much easier for her to catch up and get everything done. With her own hard work and heavenly help, she learned to drive, earned straight A's, completed her difficult honors chemistry coursework, and made many new friends. I choose to believe that she kept everything balanced because, as President Nelson says, "the Lord loves effort."[66] She worked hard and Jesus Christ helped her through the power of the priesthood.

Bear's blessing talked about how he would be kind to other students and look out for people who needed a friend, which he might have done regardless. But, early in the school year, an unexpected opportunity allowed him to work as a peer tutor for middle school students with disabilities. Soon, the special needs students were stopping Bear in the hallway for high-fives and to do the custom handshakes that he created for them. I started looking forward to Bear's daily stories about what happened in his peer tutoring class. Soon, he reported that other students had signed up to help with the peer tutoring program, and the special needs kids sometimes even sat at his table during lunch. This experience impacted the way Bear felt about himself and the way others saw him at school.

Bear also became friends with a neighbor who had previously avoided him because of some Nerf wars that had gone sideways. He

---

66. President Russell M. Nelson in Joy D. Jones' "An Especially Noble Calling" *Ensign*, May 2020.

matured exponentially in his ability to get along with the girls his age who reacted to everything with more sensitivity than his male friends. I had marveled at his new ability to befriend former enemies but didn't make the connection to heaven until I read the blessing that Jeff had given him several months before.

Our youngest child, Scout, also had promises about new friends in her blessing. She had bemoaned her fate in third grade when she saw the class lists, which showed that all her close friends had been assigned to Mrs. Luka's class, while Scout's name appeared on Mrs. Munot's list. Within a few weeks, she had new best friends named Pepper and Lexi. But an even bigger blessing occurred when a new family moved into our neighborhood with a daughter Scout's age and the school assigned Ayla to Mrs. Munot's class. Scout's blessing also helped her improve her ability to focus and become a better reader.

One can argue against anything religious, right? You can pray for something to happen and when it does, someone might claim that it would have happened even without the prayer. No external evidence exists to prove it one way or the other, but the Holy Ghost testified to me that these priesthood blessings did have a significant, positive impact on my children. I felt grateful for the power of the priesthood and for Jeff as their stepdad.

* * *

Confessing God's hand in all things increases our faith because when we give credit to the Source of all blessings out loud, the Holy Ghost testifies to us that we spoke the truth. My mom does not like to speak in public. Using homemade pie and cookies as bribes, she has convinced multiple bishops and stake presidents to not ask her to speak in meetings. As a kid, I never heard my mom bear her testimony from a pulpit, but I did hear her quietly give credit to Heavenly Father for miracles and it increased my faith more than any sermon I heard in church.

Years ago, we sat in a hot Suburban in southern Utah on a family trip, waiting for my dad to change his clothes in a gas station bathroom. We had spent four days camping at Lake Powell and stopped for gas before the long drive home. Although we all felt sticky from the heat, my mom told us that my dad had felt impressed to go change out of his tank top and swim shorts and put on his garments before driving home. He didn't want to do that, but he followed the prompting immediately.

He walked out of the gas station fully dressed, and as he approached the car, he noticed something sticking up in the ski boat, which sat on a trailer connected to the Suburban. My dad climbed up onto the swim platform of the boat to secure our gear and suddenly slipped on the slick surface. It's scary for kids to watch their grown-ups fall. I had never seen my dad even trip, and now he lay on his back on the cement. I could see worry in my mom's face. It took a minute for him to get up, which he explained with, "I got the wind knocked out of me." Not finding any injuries, he climbed into the car and started driving our family home.

Exhausted from days of swimming in the sun, we sat in uncharacteristic silence, and I could hear my parents talking in the front seat. My mom said that she believed my dad was unhurt because he had his garments on. My dad agreed. I knew from the stories of the early saints and pioneers that many people were injured and even killed while wearing their garments, so I understood that my mom wasn't saying garments guarantee physical protection in every circumstance. But I marveled at how quickly my dad had acted on an unwelcome impression and because my mom gave credit to God instead of good luck, I believed that my dad's obedience brought blessings to our family that day.

* * *

Over the last ten years, I've gathered evidence that "sacrifice brings forth the blessings of heaven."[67] When we seek to align our will with God's, we put ourselves in a better position to experience miracles. During the dreaded and dreary months of January and February, Utah doesn't provide ideal weather for toddlers. Here and there, a snowy day might bring temporary fun, but for weeks on end, the bright sunshine tempts young families outside and the bitter cold sends them back in. Imperative

---

67. William W. Phelps, "Praise to the Man," *Hymns of The Church of Jesus Christ of Latter-day Saints* (Salt Lake City: The Church of Jesus Christ of Latter-day Saints, 1985).

to parental sanity, bundling up for a short excursion in the stroller brings valuable endorphins but doesn't fill the other eleven waking hours each day. Hence, the need for Neighborhood Winter Playgroup. For about five years, we opened the gym of our local church building one morning a week for any parents with babies and young kids who didn't yet attend elementary school. The kids threw balls, played tag, and raced toy cars while the parents enjoyed much-needed adult conversation.

One memorable morning, I arrived at playgroup smiling about the new relationship in my life. I had fallen in love with Jeff Matthews and hadn't told anyone beyond my immediate family yet. Another mom, Brooke Mugleston, noticed that my face beamed with news, and I decided to share my happiness with her. I had assumed she would react with surprise, since most people knew that I hadn't yet ventured on more than two official dates. But I didn't expect her to get emotional. She looked astounded and her eyes glistened. It turned out that she had a story of her own to share.

She said that a year earlier, when the stake president called her husband, Whitney, to serve as the elder's quorum president, Whitney felt ridiculously inadequate. I had great admiration for Whitney, an easygoing electrician who treated everyone like a friend. With humble honesty, he had inspired our ward when he told us from the pulpit that he had recently gotten his temple recommend and planned to never let it lapse again. He shared that he had gone a few years without one when money felt too tight for tithing, but once he qualified to do electrical work inside the temple, the miracles he experienced outweighed any financial sacrifice. I didn't know him well, but I loved him after that day.

Brooke told me that during the meeting with Whitney, the member of the stake presidency who extended the call gave him a promise. He said, "I want you to go home tonight and talk with Brooke. I want the two of you to think about five blessings that you want for your family and write them down on a piece of paper. And I promise you that by the time you are done serving as elder's quorum president, those blessings will all be granted to you."

That night, Whitney explained the situation to Brooke and told her, "I can't think of anything to ask for." They agreed that they had everything they could want, including two healthy children, a good job, a home, the gospel, and each other. Then, Whitney said, "The only thing I want is for the single moms in our ward to find good men." At that time, we had four divorced women in our ward family, including me. One of them had started dating the only single dad in our congregation, but the rest of us couldn't seem to find the time or energy to date. Brooke continued to tell me her story through her tears. She said that she and Whitney wrote the names of the three unattached single moms on a piece of paper and told the stake president the next day that the blessing they desired was for us to find righteous companions. I couldn't believe they had used that opportunity to secure blessings for other people instead of themselves.

I thought I was simply sharing happy news when I told Brooke about my relationship, but for her, I revealed a partial answer to a bold petition. As kids rode past us on toddler bikes, we talked about the other single sisters in our ward. Although we had the marital status of "divorced" in common, that didn't make us identical in personality, preference, or schedule. What were the chances we could all find healthy, happy relationships while Whitney served as the elder's quorum president?

It takes faith to ask for blessings. As we entreat, we demonstrate that at the very least, we believe in the possibility of an answer. Whitney and Brooke had enough humility to recognize the abundance of blessings in their lives and request blessings for others instead. When Brooke and I realized how our stories intersected, it strengthened her faith and mine. After that day, I continued to watch events unfold in a way that seemed "beyond good luck." Just eighteen months after Whitney and Brooke asked God to bless us instead of them, all three of the single sisters on their list had gotten remarried.

* * *

I hope the Spirit helps you remember the small and significant moments that increased your faith in Jesus Christ. If so, write down a brief synopsis before you do anything else. The starters from this chapter appear at the top of the next few pages, but feel free to skip to the blank sheets if your story doesn't answer any of those questions.

Which of God's creations has helped you feel the Spirit or increased your faith?

Have you had any experiences that increased your testimony of a particular principle of the gospel or the blessings of keeping a specific commandment?

Have you ever joined other people in praying and fasting for a common purpose? How did you feel about it?

Did a trial or difficult circumstances in your life ever build your faith in God?

Have you ever felt your testimony grow when you shared the gospel with someone else?

CHAPTER 7

Using Forms to Get Started

Let us then continue on in this important work of recording the things we do, the things we say, the things we think, to be in accordance with the instructions of the Lord. For those of you who may not have already started . . . we would suggest that this very day you begin to write your records quite fully and completely. We hope that you will do this, our brothers and sisters, for this is what the Lord has commanded.[68]

—President Spencer W. Kimball

Even if you don't feel ready to tackle a blank page yet, you can follow the counsel of many prophets and apostles "this very day," as President Kimball suggested. If you would like to warm-up before you attempt a paragraph, simply complete one of the following forms. In just a few minutes, you will have a legitimate piece of personal history! Tomorrow, if someone asks you if you keep a journal, you can proudly say, "Yes, I do."

Think of the number of forms you have completed in your lifetime. We answer questions on forms to obtain medical care, apply for a new job, ask for a loan, go on a field trip, rent an apartment, enter a contest, get into a school, participate in a sport, and take an

---

68. Spencer W. Kimball, "We Need a Listening Ear," *Ensign*, November, 1979.

extra-curricular class. Over and over, we write our address, our mother's maiden name, and the various identification and contact numbers we use.

Why not take a fraction of that time and complete a form about what matters most? When our children and grandchildren sort through our important papers someday, they might feel disappointed with only drivers' licenses and birth certificates to link them to the people they love. As you flip through the forms, imagine what you would give to have that completed questionnaire from one of your ancestors. They will smile in the spirit world when you fill it out today!

Each form creates a tangible piece of evidence that you recognized the hand of God in your life. We learn from the scriptures that physical reminders can help us remember spiritual experiences. When the Lord made it possible for the Israelites to cross the River Jordan, He wanted them to create a reminder of that miracle to help them tell their posterity what He had done for them:

> The priests that bare the ark of the covenant of the Lord stood firm on dry ground in the midst of Jordan, and all the Israelites passed over on dry ground, until all the people were passed clean over Jordan.
>
> And it came to pass, when all the people were clean passed over Jordan, that the Lord spake unto Joshua saying, Take you twelve men out of the people, out of every tribe a man, and command ye them, saying, Take you hence out of the midst of Jordan, out of the place where the priest's feet stood firm, twelve stones, and ye shall carry them over with you and leave them in the lodging place, where ye shall lodge this night.
>
> Then Joshua called the twelve men, whom he had prepared of the children of Israel, out of every tribe a man; And Joshua said unto them, Pass over before the ark of the Lord your God into the midst of Jordan, and take ye up every man of you a stone upon his shoulder, according unto the number of the tribes of the children of Israel.
>
> That this may be a sign among you, that when your children ask their fathers in time to come, saying, What mean ye by these stones?

> Then ye shall answer them, That the waters of Jordan were cut off before the ark of the covenant of the Lord; when it passed over Jordan, the waters of Jordan were cut off: and these stones shall be for a memorial unto the children of Israel forever.
>
> For the Lord your God dried up the waters of Jordan from before you, until ye were passed over, as the Lord your God did to the Red Sea, which he dried up from before us, until we were gone over.[69]

The Lord told them exactly what to do and why. He basically said, "There is a rock. Pick it up and carry it on your shoulder to help your family remember what I have done." He has likewise commanded us to record our spiritual experiences and resulting testimonies for our children and our children's children. You can create a luminous stone for them by completing one of these forms right now. President Kimball encouraged:

> **Begin today to write and keep records** of all the important things. . . . You are unique and there may be incidents in your experience that are more noble and praiseworthy in their way than those recorded in any other life. There may be a flash of illumination here and a story of faithfulness there . . . **Your story should be written now** while it is fresh and while the true details are available."[70]

First, fill out the form, *then* give that little piece of your story a title on the top line. Trust me, it's easier to think of a title once you write the story. (See chapter 10 for more on creating introductions at the end of the writing process.) If you would rather type than hand write, go to https://truestorywriting.com/forms to access editable digital forms.

---

69. Joshua 3:16–17; 4:1–7, 23.
70. Spencer W. Kimball, "The Angels May Quote From It" *Ensign,* October 1975; emphasis added.

____

TITLE

I believe that Jesus:

- ☐ is my Savior
- ☐ is my brother
- ☐ redeemed my soul
- ☐ loves me
- ☐ is my advocate with the Father
- ☐ is aware of me
- ☐ is the Son of God
- ☐ is alive today
- ☐ is the head of The Church of Jesus Christ of Latter-day Saints
- ☐ communicates with the current prophet, President ________
- ☐ other: ________________________
- ☐ other: ________________________
- ☐ other: ________________________
- ☐ other: ________________________
- ☐ other: ________________________

____

TITLE

My favorite

☐ scripture: ☐ passage: ☐ story:

____

____

____

I like it because:

____

____

____

When I:

☐ hear ☐ sing ☐ listen to

☐ read the lyrics of ☐ other________________

The:

☐ Primary song ☐ hymn

☐ other piece of music: ________________________

I:

☐ feel ☐ think ☐ know

____

____

____

____

TITLE

Sometimes, I feel God's love when I am serving others. One time, I chose to serve:

- ☐ a family member named ________________________
- ☐ a neighbor named ____________________________
- ☐ a ward member named __________________________
- ☐ my friend named _____________________________
- ☐ a stranger who I met when I was ___________________
- ☐ other: ____________________________________

I helped by:

____

____

____

After I served them, I:

- ☐ felt of God's love for __________________________
- ☐ felt of God's love for me
- ☐ experienced an increase of love toward that person
- ☐ knew that ___________________________________
- ☐ wanted to ___________________________________
- ☐ other: ____________________________________

____

TITLE

My testimony of the reality of God increased when I appreciated His creations in / at / on:

- ☐ my yard
- ☐ the park
- ☐ the desert
- ☐ the jungle
- ☐ the woods
- ☐ the prairie
- ☐ the mountains
- ☐ the beach
- ☐ other: ______________________________

I observed:

- ☐ the sky
- ☐ the ocean
- ☐ a waterfall
- ☐ the sunset
- ☐ the sunrise
- ☐ a tree: ______________________________
- ☐ a flower: ______________________________
- ☐ some wildlife: ______________________________
- ☐ a rock formation: ______________________________
- ☐ other: ______________________________

And I:

- ☐ felt
- ☐ thought
- ☐ wondered
- ☐ knew
- ☐ other: ______________________________

that / how / about:

____

____

____

____

TITLE

I once heard a general conference talk that:

- ☐ made me think about the gospel in a new way
- ☐ answered a question that I had
- ☐ helped me feel like God is aware of me
- ☐ seemed like it was written just for me
- ☐ brought me a feeling of peace and comfort
- ☐ increased my faith
- ☐ motivated me to change
- ☐ helped me understand the gospel of Jesus Christ better
- ☐ other: ____________________________________

It happened when:

- ☐ President __________________
- ☐ Elder ____________________
- ☐ Sister ____________________

of the ___________________________________ spoke during the:

- ☐ morning session
- ☐ afternoon session
- ☐ evening session

On the ____ of

- ☐ April 19____ /20____
- ☐ October 19____ /20____

During that talk, I:

- ☐ thought
- ☐ felt
- ☐ knew
- ☐ wondered
- ☐ wanted

- ☐ decided
- ☐ other: ______________________________

____

____

____

____

____

____

____

____

____

I am grateful that he / she said:

____

____

____

____

____

____

____

____

____

____

TITLE

I once had a Church leader who impacted my testimony in a positive way. This leader's name is ________________________________ and they served as my:

- ☐ Primary teacher
- ☐ Young Women leader
- ☐ Young Men leader
- ☐ Sunday School teacher
- ☐ Relief Society president
- ☐ Elder's Quorum president
- ☐ bishop
- ☐ other: ________________

in the ____________________________ Ward

Because of his / her

- ☐ example
- ☐ testimony
- ☐ talent
- ☐ attitude
- ☐ actions
- ☐ other: ____________________

I learned: ____

____

I still remember: _______________________________________

____

I am grateful for: _______________________________________

____

____

TITLE

I had the opportunity to be on the receiving end of service when I needed help with ____

____

____

The person who gave me a gift of

- ☐ time
- ☐ money
- ☐ energy
- ☐ testimony
- ☐ other: ____________
- ☐ work
- ☐ food
- ☐ listening
- ☐ other: ____________________
- ☐ other: ____________________

was named ____________________________________. He / she / they showed up and ______________________________________

____

____

____

Because of his / her / their kindness, I

____

____

____

____

____

____

TITLE

One time, I felt:

- ☐ angry
- ☐ annoyed
- ☐ misunderstood
- ☐ hurt
- ☐ invalidated
- ☐ other: ________________

When my:

- ☐ family member ______________________________
- ☐ coworker ________________________________
- ☐ neighbor ________________________________
- ☐ friend __________________________________
- ☐ other: _________________________________

Said / did this: ________________________________
____

I prayed about it and after:

- ☐ a week
- ☐ several weeks
- ☐ year
- ☐ many months
- ☐ a couple of months
- ☐ other: ______________

I felt:

- ☐ a small but important shift in my thinking
- ☐ a great amount of peace
- ☐ a calmness instead of my previous emotion
- ☐ ready to forgive ____________________________
- ☐ hope that things will get better someday
- ☐ a change of heart

- ☐ love for ______________________
- ☐ like I could let it go
- ☐ that God wanted me to ______________________
  ____
  ____
- ☐ other: ______________________
  ____
  ____
  ____

And since then, I:

____

____

____

____

____

____

____

____

____

____

____

____

____

____

____

____

____

TITLE

When I was _____ years old, I read the Book of Mormon: Another Testament of Jesus Christ. After I finished the book, I decided to pray about it.

I knelt / stood / sat:

- ☐ in my bedroom
- ☐ outside
- ☐ in my family room
- ☐ in my office
- ☐ other: __________________

And asked God if the Book of Mormon is true.

I received an answer:

- ☐ right then
- ☐ later that day
- ☐ on a different day
- ☐ over time
- ☐ other: ______________________

I felt: ____

____.

Since then, I have developed a stronger testimony of the Book of Mormon by: ____

____.

I believe that: ____

____.

____
TITLE

If I could ask my:

- ☐ grandma, ______________________________________,
- ☐ grandpa, ______________________________________,
- ☐ great-grandma, _________________________________,
- ☐ great-grandpa, _________________________________,
- ☐ mom, ____,
- ☐ dad, ____,
- ☐ other: ____

a question about their life, beliefs, or experiences, I would ask:

____

____

____

____

____

If my current or future posterity asked me that same question, I would answer:

____

____

____

____

____

____

____

TITLE

There was a season in my life when I had a big decision to make. It was in:

19____ / 20____, when I was ______ years old. I needed to

- ☐ decide between ________________________________ and ________________________________
- ☐ choose whether to ________________________________ or ________________________________
- ☐ figure out if I should ________________________________ or not.

To make my decision, I:

- ☐ talked to ________________________________.
- ☐ prayed about it.
- ☐ read ________________________________.
- ☐ other: ________________________________

One day, I got the help I needed when:

____

____

And because of that, I decided to:

____

____

____

TITLE

I believe that:

- ☐ God
- ☐ Heavenly Father
- ☐ our Father in Heaven
- ☐ our heavenly parents
- ☐ Heavenly Mother
- ☐ other: ____________________

Is / are:

- ☐ omniscient (all-knowing)
- ☐ all-loving
- ☐ all-powerful
- ☐ kind
- ☐ merciful
- ☐ forgiving
- ☐ patient
- ☐ creative
- ☐ happy
- ☐ funny
- ☐ other: ____________________

And I believe that He / She / They: ____________________

____

____

______________________________________.

When I think about Jesus Christ, I feel: ____________________

____

____

____

I believe / know that He: ________________________________
____
____
____.

CHAPTER 8

Polishing the Stones

Some of the most inspiring history comes from the diaries and journals of everyday people like you and me. We gain strength from the stories of those who have gone before. We learn how to be strong and what brings happiness and joy in our lives.[71]

—Elder Steven E. Snow

Once you have recorded a spiritual experience—with a form, from a starter question, or on a blank page—you hold a treasure in your hands. The time you spent will undoubtedly bless your life and possibly the lives of many others. Your story has immense value without any additional edits.

If you feel reluctant to share your experience with someone else due to its sacred and personal nature, simply keep it in a safe space until the Spirit prompts you to use it. However, if you want to share your story but feel that it first needs a little polishing, here are several straightforward ways to clean it up a bit and make it more compelling and memorable:

- Upgrade your verbs
- Add adjectives

---

71. Steven E. Snow, "The Sacred Duty of Record Keeping" *Ensign*, May 2019.

- Switch around the sentence
- Get feedback

As you work on your project, don't forget to pray for help, even about the smallest details. God loves details. Remember, He assigned this project to you in the first place, so He wants to help you succeed.

Upgrade Your Verbs

When we tell stories out loud, we tend to use the "be" verbs (be, is, am, are, was, were, been, being) more than we encounter them in books or online content. So, after writing a story the way you would tell it to a friend, you can easily take it to the next level by identifying and replacing some (or most) of the "be" verbs. Read your piece with a highlighter, hunting the "be" verbs. Replacing every single instance might make your writing sound awkward or too formal. You don't want to lose your voice and personality. But if you see two or three "be" verbs within a couple of sentences, pick one and swap it with a stronger verb. For example, you could replace the sentence, "When I **was** a kid, my grandpa **was** a very good whistler," with one of these:

- "When I **was** a kid, Grandpa **loved** to **whistle**."
- "When I **was** a kid, we always knew Grandpa had **arrived** when we heard whistling in the driveway."
- "When I **was** a kid, Grandpa **whistled** subconsciously and constantly."

Or go the extra mile and replace both:

- "During my childhood, Grandpa **whistled** subconsciously and constantly."
- "When I **replay** my childhood experiences in my mind, my grandpa's constant whistling **provides** the soundtrack."
- "As a kid, I **admired** my grandpa's talent for whistling."

In another example, you could replace, "My mother-in-law and I **were** finally friends" with one of these:

- "My mother-in-law and I **grew** closer that summer."
- "My mother-in-law and I finally **developed** a strong friendship."
- "My mother-in-law and I **progressed** toward the friendship I had hoped for."

Verbs other than "be" verbs also make good candidates for an upgrade. Notice how the energy in your story changes if you upgrade the verb "went," to one of these:

- Jogged
- Strode
- Skipped
- Sauntered
- Snuck

Similarly, sentences come to life when you upgrade "said" to:

- Whispered
- Commanded
- Shouted
- Announced
- Wondered
- Confided

You may wonder which verbs can effectively replace other verbs. When I wrote term papers in high school and college, I kept a green paperback thesaurus on my desk. But now, we can search for a synonym online with a single click or even with our voices. Many free websites eagerly wait to suggest alternatives to your verbs. You can just type "synonym for" and the verb you want to upgrade into any search engine.

Add Adjectives

Adding a sprinkle of adjectives makes a story more interesting. To figure out where to use extra description, imagine a curious five-year-old who loves to interrupt people when they are talking. Have you ever gone on a road trip with an insatiably curious child? At first, the enthusiastic innocence and curiosity seem charming. A few hours later, you long to complete a single sentence without a cheerful interjection. For example, if your story said, "I put the berries into a bowl," you could imagine this curious child interrupting to ask, "What *kind* of berries?"

You patiently explain, "Frozen raspberries," then begin again, "I put the frozen raspberries into a bowl."

"What *kind* of a bowl?" You get the idea. And although the imaginary conversation with this child could wear on you after some time, you have to admit that the sentence, "I put the frozen raspberries into a big Tupperware bowl," creates a more vivid image than, "I put the berries into a bowl."

As you select several nouns in your story and add an adjective to describe each one, the specifics make the experience sound real. Our brains tend to associate general terms with hypothetical situations; therefore, distinct details add validity to your story. Adjectives have the power to engage your reader mentally and emotionally, more effectively preserving your precious memories. Which version of these sentences sounds more like a true story?

- "I got hurt when I fell off a fence."
- "I broke my arm when I fell off a chain link fence."

It turns out that God is not the only one who loves details.

Switch Around the Sentence

We often arrange the parts of our sentences in the same order, sentence after sentence. Our minds expect this pattern, and it doesn't alarm or annoy a reader. However, an occasional break from the familiar order adds an element of sophistication. For example, in this story, watch for the order of the subject (the person or thing that the sentence is about), the verb (whatever the subject is doing), and the object (the thing receiving the action).

> Kate realized that she had forgotten to do her virtual chemistry lab. She immediately started panicking. She sat at the counter and opened her laptop, almost in tears. I didn't know how I could help her, so I went into my bedroom, and I said a prayer.

To make it easier to understand this pattern, here is the story with labels:

> Kate (subject) realized (verb) that she had forgotten to do her chemistry lab (object). She (subject) immediately started panicking (verb). She (subject) sat (verb) at the counter (object) and she (subject) opened (verb) her laptop (object), almost in tears. I (subject) didn't know (verb) how I (subject) could help (verb) her, so I (subject) went (verb) into my bedroom (object) and I (subject) said (verb) a prayer (object).

Starting with a verb instead of the subject often opens a way to combine two sentences into a single, more complex sentence. If we wanted to switch around the first two sentences to break up the subject-verb-object pattern, we could tell it this way:

> Realizing (verb) that she (subject) had forgotten to do her virtual chemistry lab (object), Kate (subject) immediately started panicking (verb).

Another way to switch around the sentence parts involves looking for the word "because." Looking for "because" gives you the opportunity to switch the order of cause-and-effect sentences, adding another level to your writing. For example, "I put our toothbrushes and toothpaste in the church bag **because** we were running late," can become,

"**Because** we were running late, I put our toothbrushes and toothpaste in the church bag."

In another true and unfortunate example, I can easily switch, "I volunteered to sing karaoke because the previous two performers had next to no musical ability," to say, "**Because** the previous two performers had next to no musical ability, I volunteered to sing karaoke."

Get Feedback

When we hear or read each other's stories, we often have questions about the timeline, the details, or the underlying motivations and feelings. Pick a trusted family member or friend to read your story, and encourage them to jot down any questions they have. Adding the answers to those questions will deepen your record and make it even more enjoyable to read. With this approach, you will satisfy the curiosity of your future readers and improve your story without having to figure out what to add, change, or clarify.

The following pages provide a place for you to play with some of your sentences. Practice upgrading a verb, adding an adjective, or switching around a sentence or two. Soon, you will feel ready to get some feedback about your story!

CHAPTER 9
Helping Our Kids

It is our privilege and responsibility to help children "get far enough in" to the gospel of Jesus Christ. And we cannot begin too soon . . . .we can assist children in recognizing when they are feeling the Spirit.[72]

—President Joy D. Jones

We all want our children and grandchildren to learn how to recognize the influence of the Holy Ghost in their lives. What better way to show them that spiritual experiences are real and important than to help them record those moments? In this way, we can "labor diligently to write, to persuade our children . . . to believe in Christ."[73] If a child prays for something and receives any kind of answer, write it down! If one of the youth in your family or ward shares how they received guidance or felt peace, a few minutes can capture that moment forever. As they collect their stories, kids and teenagers build a volume of personal scripture they can use throughout their lives. Elder John H. Groberg taught, "I have a strong feeling that when this life is over, our personal and family histories

---

72. Joy D. Jones, "Essential Conversations" *Liahona*, April 2021.
73. 2 Nephi 25:23.

and the influence they wield will be of much greater importance than we now think."[74]

Our daughter Scout once lamented, "I don't have a testimony!" After asking a couple of questions, I discovered that she thought the word "testimony" meant a story that someone tells from the pulpit during fast and testimony meeting. Inwardly chastising myself, I wondered how I had failed to teach my child this important definition. She has heard family members refer to testimonies and how we want to nourish them and share them, and upon further reflection, I could see why she thought "testimony" meant "personal, spiritual experience." When I explained, "A testimony is just what you believe about Heavenly Father and Jesus," she looked immensely relieved.

Soon, our Heavenly Parents blessed Scout with a spiritual experience of her own. One night, she climbed into bed and realized that she couldn't see the night light that usually provided a soft glow in her room. Just then, she noticed that she still "felt" a light in her room. When I came to tuck her into bed, she explained what had happened and I told her, "I think what you felt is the Holy Ghost, helping you feel safe." She agreed and later wrote:

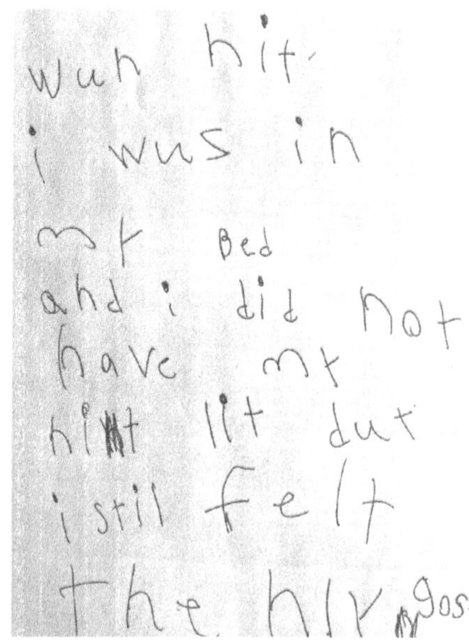
wuh hit
i wus in
my Bed
and i did not
have my
nit lit dut
i stil felt
the hly gos

74. John H. Groberg, "Writing Your Personal and Family History" *Ensign*, May 1980.

My explanation of "testimony" must not have effectively reset the definition in her mind, because Scout referred to her nightlight tender mercy as "my testimony." When we had church at home during the COVID-19 pandemic, Scout asked several times if she could share her testimony with our family. Then, she would get up, often stand on a chair or a stool, and retell that story.

The next time Scout recognized the Holy Ghost, He played a different role but again came to her at bedtime. She wanted to share with me the scripture that her Primary teacher had helped her class look up and mark in the Doctrine and Covenants. Unfortunately, Scout couldn't remember the section or verse numbers, and when I offered to search for it on the Gospel Library app, she couldn't even remember a phrase from it. I began to scan that week's Come, Follow Me lesson, but Scout said she marked this scripture "the week before last week!" As she grew increasingly frustrated, I sent a text to her teacher, and we said a prayer that we would find the verses that Scout wanted to read again. Abruptly, Scout sat up straight in bed and shouted, "Sixty-three, nine and ten! Sixty-three, nine and ten!" I wondered if that could possibly be the correct reference. We looked it up and found:

> But behold, faith cometh not by signs, but signs follow those that believe. Yea, signs come by faith, not by the will of men, nor as they please, but by the will of God.[75]

Exuberant, Scout took my phone and read the verses out loud, her eyes sparkling even in the dim bedroom. Then, she turned to me and exclaimed, "I think I have a new testimony! Because I don't think I just remembered that scripture, I think the Holy Ghost helped me remember it!" I agreed wholeheartedly and gave her a hug. Because the Spirit also prompts us to testify of truth, Scout felt a strong desire to tell someone about her exciting experience. I let her get out of bed to tell her stepdad what had happened. When I later encouraged her to write about it, Scout captured her feelings using newly learned punctuation marks (see following page):

---

75. Doctrine and Covenants 63:9–10.

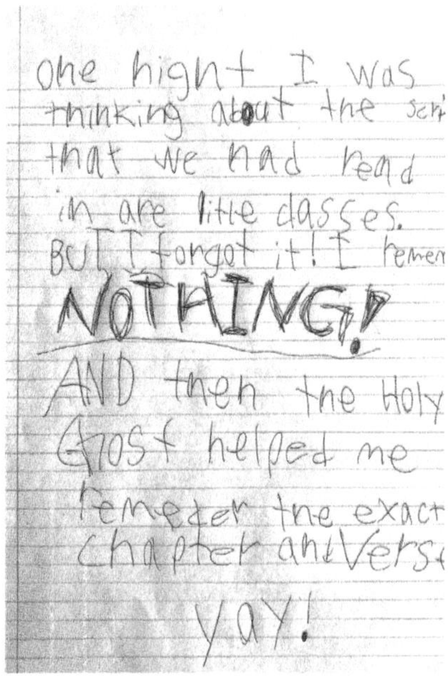

one night I was
thinking about the scri
that we had read
in are litte classes.
BUT I forgot it! I remem
NOTHING!
AND then the Holy
Ghost helped me
remeber the exact
chapter and Verse
yay!

To record their testimony-building experiences, kids with certain personalities need nothing more than a bedtime extension and a blank journal. Many others, however, might not act on the challenge without some support. You know your kids better than anyone, except for their Heavenly Parents, who will guide you if you pray and ask for help. In our family, in addition to providing paper and encouragement, we use a combination of approaches, including:

- Fun with Forms
- Exclusive Interview
- Correct Me if I'm Wrong
- Little Red Hen

Fun with Forms

Add a treat or a favorite snack to a couple of the forms in chapter 7, and you have everything you need to accomplish a family home evening that yields a valuable spiritual record. Or, if you ever find yourself searching for screen-free Sunday afternoon activities, spending twenty minutes on this project could make the Sabbath more of a delight[76] and less of a struggle. Kids encounter forms every day, but teachers call them "worksheets." The similarity to homework might play in your favor with younger kids who enjoy feeling like experts and might get excited about the novelty of using a new pen or sliding their finished form into a plastic page protector.

Teens might appreciate how the straightforward forms enable them to complete a parental request in less time than it takes to straighten up their bedrooms. And to sweeten the deal, you can always offer to substitute completed forms for certain household chores. Most of the teenagers I know would rather answer a few questions than unload the dishwasher, even though both activities take about five minutes.

Once kids complete a few of the forms, it's important to carefully save those valuable records. Although worthy of a fireproof safe, they will benefit the writer and the family more when easily accessible, so you might want to keep them in a three-ring binder, put them in a manila folder, or store them in a plastic box with a lid. Personally, I would also make a copy of each one. And put *those* in a fireproof safe.

Exclusive Interviews

Kids who resent anything that resembles extra schoolwork will prefer a verbal interview. One of my children particularly enjoys it when I ask him a series of questions about his spiritual experiences. With this approach, he doesn't have to write or type, but simply soaks up the one-on-one attention. Many kids associate being interviewed with famous people they see online or on TV. In our culture, if someone wants to write down what you say, they must think your ideas are important—exactly the message we want to send to our kids about the small and subtle experiences they have with the Spirit.

Sometimes, interviews occur spontaneously as part of casual conversations. A couple of months before her third birthday, Kate's dad wondered if she could differentiate between real people and imaginary characters, both animated and those portrayed by live actors. They had

76. Russell M. Nelson, "The Sabbath is a Delight" *Ensign*, April 2015.

this exchange, which I later recorded in my journal, along with my thoughts about it.

> DAD: Is the Big, Bad Wolf real or pretend?
> KATE: Pretend.
> DAD: Is a monster real or pretend?
> KATE: Pretend.
> DAD: Is Clifford the Big, Red Dog real or pretend?
> KATE: Pretend.
> DAD: Is Nana real or pretend?
> KATE: Real.
> DAD: Is Princess Buttercup real or pretend?
> KATE: Pretend.
> DAD: Is Berit real or pretend?
> KATE: Real.
> DAD: Is a witch real or pretend?
> KATE: Pretend.
> DAD: Is Jesus real or pretend?
> KATE: Jesus is real
>
> What a great moment. How does she know? She's never talked to Jesus and never seen Him that she remembers. She's seen paintings and pictures in books, just like she has of all the pretend characters. We tell stories of Jesus and learn about Jesus in church, but we also tell fairy tale stories and learn the names of all the Disney characters. But she still knows.

The short commentary I wrote about that conversation means a great deal to me. If I had only Kate's words, I might wonder if I had intentionally taught her those answers through repetition, like verbal flashcards. If we had practiced, my tone would have conveyed pride or satisfaction, but I sound more surprised and a little amazed, evidence that Kate connected those dots for herself. I'm grateful that I took an extra minute to record my feelings.

When you ask your kids what they learned that day in Primary, you can also ask a couple of follow-up questions to find out what they understand and believe about that gospel principle or scripture story. Likewise, if your child mentions an experience that may have included the Holy Ghost, you can conduct a simple interview with a few specific questions. And even if they don't provide you with an obvious opportunity, you can ask them one of the starter questions from chapters 2–6 or use one of the forms from chapter 7 as a script for your interview.

Kids talk fast and it's best for the conversation to flow as naturally as possible, so unless you type like lightning, using a voice memo app on your phone or a stand-alone voice recorder will help you capture all the details they notice and remember, in phrases that you would never say the same way your child does. When I typed up this interview from a voice recording, I captured my eleven-year-old's personality and simple faith about finding his elusive pet tortoise (over and over):

MOM: Can you think of a time when you have felt the Holy Ghost?

BEAR: Sure. Whenever I find Oogway, once a week.

MOM: And what does that feel like?

BEAR: Like I know that I am going to find him. I don't know what people are talking about with this "warm blanket" hibbity jibbity. It feels like someone cracks an egg inside of you and then you know what's going to happen.

MOM: You're good at praying for Oogway when he is lost.

BEAR: I've had a lot of practice.

MOM: Have you had any other prayers answered that weren't about your lost pet?

BEAR: I prayed for Andrew's dad, Matt. And I think that worked out OK. How's he doing?

One of the most valuable aspects of the interview approach comes from the way our brains make connections as we talk. Your teenager or child might not realize that the Holy Ghost gave them an idea or feeling until they explain their experience out loud. Interview questions can lead to epiphanies. Depending on how the conversation evolves, you may even feel a prompting from the Spirit to ask, "Do you think that maybe the Holy Ghost helped you?"

Correct Me if I'm Wrong

Providing almost constant contrast to her brother, my busy teenage daughter doesn't enjoy the novelty of being interviewed, regarding it as slightly inefficient and kind of silly. For her, I use an approach that I call Correct Me if I'm Wrong. She does some journaling on her own, but when life gets busy with debate tournaments, chemistry tests, and the hunt for a perfect prom dress, writing about a spiritual experience sinks lower and lower on her to-do list. Before it completely disappears, I like to take a quick stab at whatever story she shared with me.

For example, Kate and her friend Kennedy had gotten into a complicated and painful misunderstanding that lasted several weeks. I knew that Kate hoped to clear the air, so I felt intrigued when she shared that the Holy Ghost gave her an idea about how to navigate the reconciliation. As per the prompting she received, Kate made a list and invited Kennedy to go on a walk. Afterward, Kate happily reported in the kitchen that they had resolved the conflict. Elated, I typed up a quick summary of her experience in less time than it takes to fold a load of laundry, then printed it out and asked her to review my paragraph to see if I missed anything or if I even came close to describing the event as she experienced it. She eagerly identified the errors and filled in the gaps.

How often do parents ask their children to correct them? Some teenagers will relish the opportunity to evaluate and improve upon something that their mom or dad created, especially if they get praised and thanked for it. Sometimes it works well for a parent to author the main story and then let the teenager add a few quotes to bring it to life by including their personality. When I had a starting draft ready, Kate and I worked together for a few minutes to create a version that included her actual words, which she allowed me to record since I wasn't asking her any interview questions and she could just talk freely. I know the final version will help her in years to come when she has conflict with college roommates, mission companions, coworkers, or a spouse:

> We all prayed that Kate's talk with Kennedy, their first one-on-one conversation in weeks, would go well. And it went so much better than we could have expected! Kate found out that Kennedy wasn't *trying* to get her in trouble. Kennedy had a

video where Kate said something unkind about our neighbor and without even thinking, Kennedy shared a clip from the video with someone, who passed it along. But now, they have both apologized and decided they can still be friends! They even agreed to help each other break their bad habit of gossiping.

The best part was when Kate gave the Holy Ghost credit for the idea of making a list of all the reasons she loves being friends with Kennedy. She told Jeff and I at the counter, "so, #churchgirl moment . . . I prayed about what to do about Kennedy and then as I was falling asleep, the thought came to me to write a list of things I liked about her as a friend!" I was so happy that she recognized that as personal revelation! Even in her bedtime prayer that night, she said to Heavenly Father, "thank you for giving me the idea to . . ."

The next day, when I asked Kate about how her talk with Kennedy went, she described the prompting from the Holy Ghost as a, "two-birds-with-one-stone kind of dealio because once I made the list, that put in my head all the things I liked about Kennedy, which made me not as rude when I talked to her. And number two, when Kennedy felt like total crap during our conversation, I'm like, 'I have a list for you!' And then she's all touched and happy. I'm glad the Holy Ghost could have influenced me to make a smart decision amidst all of this drama and help me save a friendship."

Little Red Hen

In the American fable of the Little Red Hen, a chicken tries to enlist the help of other animals as she plants and harvests wheat, grinds flour, and makes bread. At the end of each step, when the other farmyard animals refuse to contribute their time or energy, she concludes, "I will do it myself." As much as I love collaborating with my kids to record their spiritual experiences, some moments will simply get lost and forgotten unless I do it myself. Thankfully, even if you use this approach, you won't have to enjoy the hot, fresh bread all alone the way the Little Red Hen did! You can choose to share the meaningful results of your work and others will enjoy the blessings.

A Little Red Hen project can start with something as simple as jotting down a few things your kids or grandkids say in their prayers. They help us remember to express gratitude for our blessings, such as when my daughter prayed, "And we thank thee that there is a system where we can go and borrow books for free." I hadn't taken the time to thank God for public libraries, though I probably should have. Even basic gospel truths sound fresh and new when kids state them with sincere enthusiasm. After we talked about the plan of salvation, a seven-year-old Kate exclaimed, "The reward is HUGE! It's so big. And what He asks is easy." If you write it down, a single sentence can supply spiritual nourishment to their testimonies—and yours—for years.

When I was expecting a new baby, Kate asked if we could pray and ask Heavenly Father for our baby to be a certain gender. I explained that our baby had already developed into a boy or girl and just hadn't grown big enough for a doctor to tell yet. She responded, "But Heavenly Father will give us what is best for our family, right?" Her faith amazed me. As I answered, "Yes, He will," the Holy Ghost testified to me that I had spoken the truth. And so had Kate. She had no idea how much it helped me to have a reassurance that God knows what we need.

When we have "simple yet essential conversations with our children,"[77] we can write down some of the things they say. In addition to reminding us of the truths we teach them, kids often make connections or look at the gospel in ways we have never considered. When Bear first learned about Alma's analogy that compares faith to a seed,[78] he asked, "Do some people have a testimony that is like a redwood?" Before that moment, each time I heard that verse from the Book of Mormon, I pictured emerging pea plants from my junior high biology class, so his question caught me off guard. I considered for a moment, then testified to him that the scriptures contain true accounts of people with faith that was unshakable,[79] so they must have grown their seeds of faith into redwoods. "That's what I'm going to do," he decided. Because I recorded his epiphany, that motivating

---

77. Joy D. Jones, "Essential Conversations" *Liahona*, April 2021.
78. Alma 32:28.
79. Jacob 7:5.

comparison became part of Bear's lexicon. Seven years later, he continues to visualize and strive for faith of that magnitude.

If we are humble, we can learn from the smallest disciples because "little children do have words given unto them many times."[80] In fourth grade, Kate wondered how to reconcile evolution with the biblical account of creation. After thinking and praying about it for weeks, she arrived at her own conclusion. One night, as I tucked her into bed, she told me that she had decided religion and science "are like a smoothie," because Jesus Christ used both, blending priesthood power and scientific laws to create the earth. With that hypothesis, my young scientist began her lifelong quest to balance dichotomous truths.

Even comments that make us laugh can provide valuable glimpses into what a child believes. It made my day to hear Scout offhandedly remark, "I think of Heavenly Father and Jesus as being all glowing and perfect. But I bet Heavenly Mother is *funny*." I couldn't help but smile at her tone which implied that "perfect" does not equal the ultimate compliment. Maybe the countless examples of imperfection in her earthly mother have helped her imagine Heavenly Mother as approachable. I can only hope for silver linings like that.

When kids are too young to journal for themselves, we can create single-sentence records that will warm our hearts and build our faith. In other cases, the complexity or length of a particular story might necessitate the Little Red Hen approach. When Bear experienced a miracle in second grade, his age and emotional proximity to the story precluded him from writing it or even telling it with the detail I wanted to preserve for "the learning and the profit of my children."[81] Many of our children's experiences include and impact other family members, especially their parents. Even though this tender mercy happened to Bear, I witnessed it, and it deepened my faith in Jesus Christ.

After hearing family members talk about school shootings and other concerning news stories, eight-year-old Bear had a difficult time going to school and an even harder time falling asleep at night. He spent at least an hour every evening crying, whimpering, and panicking. For a while, he begged for a parent to check on him every five

---

80. Alma 32:23.
81. 2 Nephi 4:15.

to ten minutes. Then, we had a few extremely draining and alarming nights when Bear tearfully pleaded for me to check on him every three minutes. He could calm down while I sang or prayed, but as soon as I left the room, he immediately panicked again. I have never seen him so agitated and afraid.

His fear of being murdered had gone on for quite a while, even though we tried to coach him on how he had the ability to control his thoughts. Meeting with the school counselor helped for a brief time, but if either of his parents had to travel for work, Bear's anxiety flared up again. Although he logically knew that he was safe, he still felt more fear than I have ever felt or witnessed in another person.

Before general conference weekend, I asked each person in our family to identify one or two questions and suggested that we pray to receive the answers as we listened to the speakers and paid attention to the whisperings of the Holy Ghost. The kids had never tried this before, and I had no idea what to expect. Bear didn't hesitate to share his question: "How can I not be so afraid?"

On April 2, 2017, we were watching the Sunday afternoon session of conference at my parents' house. Bear listened to most of the talks in another room with his aunt Jessie, but during the first part of then-President Dieter F. Uchtdorf's talk, he walked into the kitchen where I sat at the counter. I had already written one sentence in my journal that President Uchtdorf had said, and I told Bear, "Read this!" I kept writing as Bear's favorite apostle continued with sentence after sentence about how to overcome fear with faith and how the pure love of Christ can conquer fear. When he testified that we do not need to be afraid about things that may or may not happen, I told Bear, "I just saw your prayer being answered. Just now." It amazed me how not only did an entire conference talk address Bear's concern, but it happened during a moment when my energetic little boy wasn't jumping on the tramp, playing in the basement, or rolling around on the couch. He listened to a lot of conference talks but also missed quite a few talks when he couldn't hold still. But he heard the one that he needed, and I truly felt like I had witnessed a miracle. President Uchtdorf said:

> Therefore, let us set aside our fears and live instead with joy, humility, hope, and a bold confidence that the Lord is with us.

> My beloved friends, my dear brothers and sisters in Christ, if we ever find ourselves living in fear or anxiety, or if we ever find that our own words, attitudes, or actions are causing fear in others, I pray with all the strength of my soul that we may become liberated from this fear by the divinely appointed antidote to fear: the pure love of Christ, for "perfect love casteth out fear."
>
> Christ's perfect love gives us the confidence to press through our fears and place our complete trust in the power and goodness of our Heavenly Father and of His Son, Jesus Christ. In our homes, in our places of business, in our Church callings, in our hearts, let us replace fear with Christ's perfect love. Christ's love will replace fear with faith![82]

I couldn't believe that Bear received such a clear answer. But what happened next surprised us even more. That answer to prayer had an immediate and noticeable impact. The bedtime routine on Sunday night went better, and so did Monday night. He went to his dad's, who reported that bedtime felt calmer, and soon Bear had accomplished a five-day streak of not crying at night.

I wanted to apply President Uchtdorf's message in tangible ways. A couple of days after conference, I had an idea to put several pictures of Christ and quotes from the talk on Bear's ceiling, where he could easily see them from his loft bed. Handing him a small flashlight, I instructed him to look at the pictures and quotes if he got scared during the night. Before conference, when Bear would ask me what he should think about at night, I had been suggesting animated kids movies for him to replay in his mind, but after conference, I started suggesting specific scripture stories about Jesus that Bear could envision and imagine in detail as he waited for his body to fall asleep.

I told Bear that miracles take work and that he would have to continue to put forth effort to change his thoughts. I reminded him of how hard Nephi worked to build a boat, even though God enabled

---

82. President Dieter F. Uchtdorf, "Perfect Love Casteth Out Fear" *Ensign*, April 2017.

him to do it.[83] With the Lord's help, Bear worked to change, and his transformation astounded us. He had wanted to conquer his fears for weeks. Anxious for a solution, he had asked me multiple times through frustrated and fearful tears, "How can I get better?" Now he knew how, and when he felt afraid, he focused on Jesus Christ.

On April 10, Bear fell asleep silently, completely calm, and quiet. He drifted off so quickly that I wished I had a recording of the hour between when he got in bed and when he fell asleep just a week and a half prior. I had no doubt that we had experienced a miracle.

A few nights later, Bear woke up from a nightmare and described his dream to me, saying, "Someone took me and then you and Dad stopped him, but he came back and shot everyone." Although inwardly appalled at the images that filled his subconscious, I reassured him that he was safe and suggested that he go back into that picture in his mind and visualize a different ending. I thought it might work better to create an alternate story than to just abandon the nightmare and hope the dream did not recur. I walked him through some possibilities, such as picturing the guy shooting a Nerf gun at everyone or seeing President Uchtdorf arrive and help tie up the bad guy with duct tape. Bear loved that suggestion and thanked me before going back to sleep for the rest of the night.

I felt like an ancient Israelite woman or a Nephite mother who had witnessed the Savior heal her child. I wanted to tell everyone I knew. One morning, gratitude compelled me to tell the school secretaries what had had happened. They listened quietly, then said they had also noticed a change in Bear's demeanor and his ability to come to school and stay in his classroom all day without calling home. I testified of the power of Jesus Christ and thanked them for allowing me to share our story.

* * *

Our kids, grandkids, nieces, nephews, and youth in our wards experience small and big miracles. Let's help them get even further into the gospel of Jesus Christ by giving credit where credit is due. You can use the next few pages to conduct your own exclusive interview with one of the children in your life. If you have a young family member

83. 1 Nephi 17:8–16, 50–51, 18:1–4.

who might enjoy adding to or editing your version of their experience, additional pages have room for you to experiment with that approach. If you are going the Little Red Hen route, please remember that you are not ever really doing it all by yourself, because the Lord is with you in this holy work. When we consider what He has done for us and for our kids, we might realize that we have a "new testimony," one that might even include exclamation marks.

CHAPTER 10
Ending with the Introduction

Having seen many afflictions in the course of my days, nevertheless, having been highly favored of the Lord in all my days; yea, having had a great knowledge of the goodness therefore I make a record of my proceedings in my days.[84]

—Nephi, son of Lehi

You did it! You recorded a spiritual experience by starting in the middle of your story. It may not even need a formal introduction. You may choose to give it a title (or not), but regardless, make sure to include your full name and date somewhere on the document, whether in a subtitle, a header, or a footer at the bottom of the page. We tend toward unrealistic optimism when it comes to remembering the year that a significant event occurred, and even if we can accurately place a story on a timeline, our children and grandchildren will need those details.

If you would also like to add a little more context to lead into your story, that makes a perfect final step to this piece of your project. It seems counterintuitive to write the introduction at the end, but it saves you stress and benefits your blood pressure. Remember the daunting blank page? Now it contains your story, and you can easily create a succinct opener or a powerful prequel. Both approaches have

84. 1 Nephi 1:1.

wonderful examples straight from the scriptures, the best collection of recorded spiritual experiences that we have.

Succinct Openers

Nephi provided us with the ultimate example of a brief introduction in The Book of Mormon: Another Testament of Jesus Christ. He planned to share several spiritual experiences, and he didn't use any paragraphs on unnecessary backstory. By verse five, someone in his family interacts with the Lord and the action begins. So, what does Nephi provide in the first four verses? He doesn't waste time or get off track by introducing each person in his family, although I would have personally felt tempted to give the reader a heads-up about my older brothers. However, that would have started the story with a negative tone and created a distraction from the upcoming luminous stone. Instead, Nephi simply tells us his name, that he has had some consequential ups and downs, and that he believes in Jesus Christ. We can follow the same approach.

Anticipating that some skeptical readers would question the validity of his story, Nephi also testifies, "And I know that the record which I make is true; and I make it with my own hand; and I make it according to my knowledge."[85] We tend to bear our testimonies at the end of a talk, a lesson, or an email to a loved one. However, if we share our testimony in the beginning, we invite the Spirit, who can then influence the listener or reader.

As a college student in Logan, Utah, I attended an institute class taught by a faithful and knowledgeable teacher. I respected him and enjoyed his lessons, which always concluded with his fervent testimony of Jesus Christ and The Book of Mormon. One day, he grew serious, telling the class that we needed to change our behavior. Silently, everyone listened to this unexpected and somber announcement. He said that he knew we had other classes to get to and that quite a few of us had a decent walk across campus. But without realizing it, many of the students had started packing up their backpacks as soon as he said, "I would like to bear my testimony." The shuffling of papers and shifting in chairs detracted from the Spirit and made him feel that his testimony did not even reach our

85. 1 Nephi 1:3.

ears, let alone our hearts. Of course, we felt badly about our collective lack of reverence and quickly altered our Pavlov response to the cue that class would end within a couple of minutes. From then on, we listened to this good man's testimony without preparing for our departure from his classroom.

Years later, I taught a youth Sunday School class in the days when we held sacrament meeting at the end of our three-hour meeting block. Half of the class held the Aaronic Priesthood and needed to leave class ten or fifteen minutes early to go prepare the sacrament. I soon noticed that they would not be with us for the conclusion of the lesson each week. Remembering my institute teacher, I decided to begin each lesson with my testimony instead of waiting until the end. Although we often invited the Holy Ghost during our opening prayer, starting the discussion with my testimony changed the feeling in our classroom. In a similar way, starting your story with your testimony will likely change the way someone feels as they read it, even if that future reader is you.

After telling us his name and sharing his testimony, Nephi sets the stage for his true story. Again, he keeps these facts minimal, providing just enough information to keep us from getting confused or distracted as we read about Lehi's sacred experience in verse six. It might help to think of your story as a scene in a play, where your introduction contains the opening lines of the narrator. Before the curtain comes up, tell the audience where they are and who they will see when the action starts. Nephi does this by saying:

> For it came to pass in the commencement of the first year of the reign of Zedekiah, king of Judah (my father, Lehi, having dwelt in Jerusalem in all his days); and in that same year, there came many prophets, prophesying unto the people that they must repent or that great city Jerusalem must be destroyed.[86]

In a single verse, Nephi explained when this story happened, the name of the person who will pick up the first luminous stone, and what led up to the experience he wants to share. You can provide the same

86. 1 Nephi 1:4.

information in a more casual tone with more modern words. For example, in the story about my mom watching a manta ray, she might include an introduction like, "In the summer of 1998, we went on a sailing trip with our high school friends off the coast of the Windward Islands." Knowing which couple couldn't make the trip and how long everyone in the group had known each other would not add helpful context for the scuba diving experience that helped her feel close to her Creator.

If you have written about several firsthand experiences, you might notice a common thread running through them. If so, you might choose to introduce that theme in the introduction. Alternatively, you could start with a teaser, challenging the reader to look for a pattern as they learn from your stories. Have you ever noticed that people hear different themes during general conference? As the Holy Ghost teaches each one of us in our minds and hearts, we hear the instructions that apply to our lives. I remember attending a family dinner during conference weekend and remarking about how much I loved the way so many speakers had focused their talks on peace. My sister-in-law started to laugh and said, "I thought the theme of this conference was parenting!" We had each heard the messages that we needed most. The same might happen with the descendants or friends who read your stories.

As early as elementary school, we completed assignments that involved reading a paragraph and identifying the main idea. If you can summarize the main idea of your story in a single statement, that makes a great introduction. This type of opener often only takes one sentence, such as, "The summer I turned twenty-six, I had an experience that changed my testimony," or "I always wondered if going on ministering visits could really make a difference until one day, I found out for sure." It might also work well to ask a question that your story answers as it unfolds.

As you craft a simple introduction, remember to follow Nephi's example, and keep the backstory brief. You only need to include the information that the reader needs to understand and appreciate your spiritual experience. Let your story shine for itself!

Powerful Prequels

Have you ever read a book or watched a movie and found one of the characters so interesting that you want to know more of their backstory?

Sometimes, authors or directors create prequels, or stories about events that occurred before an existing narrative. While sequels tell what happened next, prequels go back in time and explain the circumstances and decisions that shaped characters' personalities and relationships. I find prequels a fascinating storytelling method, so I started to look for them in the scriptures.

Well-known scripture stories often center around dramatic moments of personal revelation and miracles. Inspired by these accounts of faith, artists create paintings of those moments, parents tell them to their children, and songwriters include references to them in Primary songs. But the prequels—the passage leading up to the classic scripture stories—contain especially instructive information. While we will never see pictures of those moments in the gospel art book, we can learn from them what to include in our own introductions. Scripture stories that showcase moments of great faith come after prequels about small, significant choices.

Before Nephi got the plates, before he broke his bow, before he built a ship, a pivotal conversation occurred. We can read this prequel in the fourth chapter of The Book of Mormon. Laman and Lemuel expressed concern because they had to get a valuable set of plates from a powerful man who wanted to kill them. This assignment came from God, but they still felt anxious about the outcome. They asked, "How is it possible that the Lord will deliver us?" revealing their doubt in the power of Jesus Christ. They worried because Laban was a "mighty man" who could "command fifty, yea, even . . . slay fifty."[87]

At that moment, Nephi encountered what many of us experience—startling, discouraging information. People in his life listed facts that could have undermined his faith. How did Nephi choose to respond?

1. He acknowledged the information. He didn't argue about whether Laban had power and influence, but instead referred to "Laban and his fifty"[88] like his brothers did. Because he didn't get defensive about that detail, he could shift the focus to more important points.

---

87. 1 Nephi 3:31.
88. 1 Nephi 4:1.

2. He looked to the scriptures and likened them unto himself by saying, "Let us be strong like unto Moses "[89] and "the Lord is able to deliver us, even as our fathers, and destroy Laban, even as the Egyptians."[90]
3. He remembered personal spiritual experiences and then reminded his brothers of their own, saying, "An angel hath spoken unto you."[91]
4. He focused on Jesus Christ and bore testimony that "the Lord . . . is mightier than all the earth."[92]
5. Even though they were "yet wroth, and did still continue to murmur," Nephi moved forward! We know that he started walking because he reports, "They did follow me up until we came without the walls of Jerusalem."[93]

Nephi had to listen to people express angry, resentful complaints and doubts on a regular basis, but he didn't let their opinions or their facts stop him from obeying the Lord. Knowing that he had to deal with potentially faith-weakening input makes his later stories more applicable to us. If the story started in 1 Nephi 4:5, as they creep into the city by night, we might mistakenly assume that Nephi went into this difficult mission buoyed up by emotional support and pep talks. While the main story contains memorable action, the prequel contains valuable instruction.

Before the brother of Jared made sixteen small stones, before he saw the Lord face-to-face, before he crossed the ocean, what did he do? In his prequel, he "dwelt in tents upon the seashore for the space of four years."[94] During that time, the brother of Jared chose every day whether to pray. And when the Lord chastised him for three hours "because he remembered not to call upon the name of the Lord,"[95] he had an opportunity to choose how he would react to receiving correction. We learned that he

89. 1 Nephi 4:2.
90. 1 Nephi 4:3.
91. 1 Nephi 4:3.
92. 1 Nephi 4:1.
93. 1 Nephi 4:4.
94. Ether 2:13.
95. Ether 2:14.

changed his habits and "repented of the evil which he had done"[96] the same way we can.

While you won't see a large oil painting of the brother of Jared camping and not praying on a beach, that information adds power to his story. Later, he testifies, "Behold, O Lord, thou canst do this. We know that thou art able to show forth great power, which looks small unto the understanding of men."[97] Without the prequel, we would know him only as one who had great faith; with the prequel, we know him as one who gained great faith by repenting and creating better habits around daily prayer.

Before you received revelation, before you felt God's love, before you followed a prompting, you made small, significant choices that put you on a trajectory to have a spiritually defining experience. If you include a few sentences about the decisions that propelled you toward that moment, your story has a better chance of directing those who come after you to find their own miracles. For example, in the story about how Whitney and Brooke Mugleston blessed multiple families with their faith, I shared a tiny prequel: the decision they made to pay tithing on a tight budget. That act of obedience led to a temple recommend, which led to tender mercies in the temple. They made life-changing choices before they witnessed life-changing events.

If you prayed, fasted, went to the temple, ministered to others, or studied the scriptures before you experienced the miracle in your story, include that information in the introduction. Powerful prequels help us connect the dots between obedience and blessings.

* * *

The next few pages provide space for you to experiment with introductions. If you still feel unsure about how to introduce your sacred record, consider the suggestions in the "Get Feedback" section of chapter 8. A family member or friend who has not read your story before will likely ask just the right question to help you figure out what to include in the introduction.

---

96. Ether 2:15.
97. Ether 3:5.

CHAPTER 11

Watching the Path

Follow the promptings that you receive. Act upon them. Like the cairns on a trail less traveled, the Holy Ghost will show you all things you should do. He will teach and testify of Christ.[98]

—President Elaine S. Dalton

As we hike up a trail, my kids are more likely to see interesting rocks if they look for them. Similarly, we will notice more miracles along the covenant path if we open our minds and hearts to the possibility of God's influence in our lives. When my brother wrote home from the mission field in Ukraine, asking us to share our spiritual experiences, our family started to consciously watch for moments when the Holy Ghost touched our minds and hearts. We noticed many more blessings and promptings after that. While the acts of receiving personal revelation and recording personal revelation can occur independently, combining them amplifies and illuminates our communication with God.

Writing about moments when we feel loved, receive instructions, or increase our faith creates a two-way dialogue with our Father in Heaven. No longer do we just talk to Him; we actively listen and create evidence that we received a response. In so doing, we "preserve

98. Elaine S. Dalton, "Come Let Us Go Up to the Mountain of the Lord," *Ensign*, May 2009.

that memory," as President Eyring said, for a future time when we need "to remember how much God loves us and how much we need Him."[99]

I didn't realize that anyone in my family had forgotten what God has done for us until my daughter, Kate, read an early draft of chapter 9. To my surprise, when she read the story about her reconciliation with Kennedy, she said, "I totally forgot about that! I mean, I remember that we were upset and that we went on a walk and talked about it. And now that you say it, I remember that I made a list of things I liked about her. But I didn't remember that I prayed about it or that it was the Holy Ghost who gave me the idea." Even though a couple of years had passed, I still couldn't believe how the subtle but significant influence of the Spirit had turned into a forgotten detail. I felt grateful for the simple, single-page document that "enlarged the memory"[100] of my daughter.

I have learned more than once that if I spot an unusual rock and don't take the time to pick it up right then, I probably won't see it again. When we receive personal revelation and procrastinate our reaction, it might not take years for that moment to fade or disappear. It can happen in mere hours! Elder Neal A. Maxwell counseled:

> A special thought can also be lost later in the day in the rough and tumble of life. God should not, and may not, choose to repeat the prompting if we assign what was given such a low priority as to put it aside.[101]

I don't know what would have happened if my dad had woken up one morning with the thought that he should sell his dream home and not chosen to pay attention. If he had brushed it aside and gone to work, would conference calls have crowded out the quiet prompting? Would the divine instruction have returned the next morning?

---

99. Henry B. Eyring, "O Remember, Remember" *Ensign*, November 2007.
100. Alma 37:8.
101. *The Neal A. Maxwell Quote Book*, ed. Cory H. Maxwell (Salt Lake City: Bookcraft, 1997), 171.

In some stages of our lives, we experience more "rough and tumble," than in others, but Satan can always find a way to distract or confuse us. John Bytheway wrote:

> It's interesting that Satan often makes his appearance after great spiritual experiences. He wants us to discount, dismiss, and explain away any event that has drawn us closer to God. . . . It would be helpful for each of us to be aware of this particular strategy of Satan . . . .when we taste the fruit of the tree of life and are filled with joy, we might be wary that Satan will try to get us to rethink or dismiss it.[102]

I once experienced a tender mercy that no one else witnessed. No outward change or event occurred, and I know without a doubt that if I had not written a journal entry about it, I would have forgotten that moment by now. When the Spirit whispers to my mind, if I don't have time to handwrite or type up the experience, I will dictate a verbal journal entry with a voice memo app. Later, I play a little game of Mad Gab with myself to decipher the text-to-speech errors. No matter how many times I journal about doing temple *sealings*, my phone will always think I had an amazing experience doing *ceilings*. But at least the message from the Holy Ghost will not get blurred or lost!

When we couldn't attend church in-person during the COVID-19 pandemic, our family held church in our basement. We kept it simple and short but gave the kids an opportunity to conduct, give talks, and lead the music. Kate particularly enjoyed typing up a printed program for our "ward" and distributing the folded sheets of paper as we entered our homemade "chapel." We built a podium by draping a tablecloth over stacked boxes and did our best to invite the Spirit into the meeting. With tiny plastic cups in a mini-muffin tray for the sacrament, the ordinance had more meaning and significance than ever before. With all the familiar routines disrupted, we looked at our worship with fresh eyes.

---

102. John Bytheway, *Lifestyles of the Great and Spacious* (Salt Lake City: Deseret Book, 2013).

However, the novelty of doing church at home came to a crashing halt as Easter Sunday approached. During the week leading up to Easter, we had done our annual Easter family home evening, opening colorful plastic eggs to reveal symbols of the Easter story. We had shared our "Jerusalem dinner," sitting on the floor and eating fish, flatbread, lentils, and grape juice. Now, the weekend approached, and the kids couldn't stop talking about the extended family traditions that had been cancelled by quarantine. We all felt disappointed when we thought about a quiet holiday instead of a weekend filled with cousins, brunch, grandparents, new dresses, and "He Is Risen" on the organ. Kate especially loved Easter Sunday and wished we could gather with our ward family and celebrate the Resurrection with inspiring musical numbers.

Jeff and I tried to think of a way we could commemorate this high and holy day within the constraints of the mandate that called for everyone to stay home and only interact with members of their own household. When he came up with the idea to have Kate plan a special Easter service, she jumped at the suggestion. Soon, we all had assignments. Scout practiced "He Is Risen" on a small instrument called a melodica, which combines elements of an accordion with a harmonica. I do not play the piano but worked on learning "Christ the Lord Is Risen Today" from the *Hymns Made Easy* book.

Although Jeff wanted to host his adult kids on Easter, he tried to be sensitive to the rules of the "stay home, stay safe" directive. I knew that quarantine brought challenges for everyone in our community but felt jealous of families who lived in the same house all the time. We constantly dealt with the tension of having members of our household go back and forth to their other homes. Each household defined lockdown differently, and everyone seemed extra sensitive and wary of the risks of each other's relatives. I knew it felt unfair to Jeff that my kids didn't want his kids to come in and out of our house but felt okay with their dad's girlfriend hanging out at their other house. Although they cited how she worked from home and didn't go out socially, logic didn't erase the hurt of inconsistency.

Focusing on solutions, Jeff invited his kids to have a Zoom call on Easter and eat their traditional meal together virtually. Everyone agreed that we could sit in four different houses with laptops and tablets and at least talk to each other while we ate. It sounded kind of fun to eat together over Zoom, since everyone would make the same dish, an open-faced toast and egg sandwich called an "Egg-la-Daisy." To make it even easier for them to keep up the family tradition, Jeff offered to drop off the ingredients at each house the day before. After buying duplicate groceries, he delivered them to Taylor's family, Dax's family, and to his former wife's house, where Allie and LJ would spend the day. For a moment, our Easter plans seemed manageable, and we felt hopeful.

Then, things got complicated, as they often do when combining two family cultures and traditions. Jeff suggested that we invite his kids to join our Easter church service over Zoom before eating the Egg-la-Daisies. Kate seemed a little worried about how that might play out but agreed to text her step-siblings and invite them to contribute talks, prayers, or songs. Busy with their full-time jobs and toddlers, Jeff's kids did not text back. I wondered if they even wanted to *watch* our Easter service, let alone participate in it. But in case the grandkids wanted to sing a Primary song or say a little prayer, we asked Kate to wait and not finalize the printed program. A few more hours went by, and still no one responded to her message. To further complicate the situation, the parenting time schedule had Kate, Bear, and Scout spending the night before Easter at their dad's house, so she left on Saturday evening with the program still up in the air.

The next morning, Jeff and I woke up to an empty house on Easter because all our kids woke up at their other parents' homes. I didn't feel sad, though, because I had one of the best antidotes to missing my kids: a project! And even better than a project, I had come up with an Easter surprise that I knew they would love. I collected leftover sheets of colored tissue paper from our craft box and our wrapping paper stash and took all the pieces outside with scissors and tape.

Carefully, I spent two hours creating a mock stained-glass window with tissue paper shapes. I cut thin gray paper into the shape of an empty tomb with a stone rolled away and then arranged long paper rectangles stretching out from the tomb like rays of the sun, alternating yellow, pink, purple, and white. A light breeze introduced an additional challenge because the tissue paper pieces kept blowing around while I tried to tape them down. Because I didn't want to get caught,

I kept pausing my work to run inside and see if the kids had arrived through the back door.

We live in a split-level home, so the outside of the window sat at ground level and the sun shone through it into our basement family room. I planned to pull down the blackout shade so no one would see the stained-glass window until they walked into our "chapel." Over and over, I taped a few pieces, then ran in the house and down the stairs to see how it looked from the other side. As I worked to cover the entire window with minimal overlap, I focused on varying the colors and cutting the pieces to fit. I couldn't remember the last time I had gotten completely absorbed in designing something tangible. It felt good to my brain to think about a single process and stay in the moment when so often, my mind dashes back and forth between thoughts of the past and plans for the future. As I created art to honor Jesus Christ, my heart filled with joy, even though it looked completely amateur and homemade. I knew that the sunshine and the Spirit would bring the colors to life and the kids would love the image for what it represented.

Unfortunately, when the kids came back from their dad's house, the mood in our house shifted from anticipation to stress. Transitions usually feel hard, but holidays seem extra touchy. Kate still hadn't heard from any step-siblings, the printer wouldn't work, and I had forgotten to charge the portable speaker, adding to her anxiety. Jeff's kids all joined the Zoom call as I realized I couldn't even play the songs from my phone because I had signed out of my music app so that Scout could access it from another device, and I couldn't remember my password. We decided to just sing acapella, and during an awkward moment of hesitation, Jeff's former wife, an accomplished quartet performer, gave us a starting note from off-screen at her house. I saw Kate's eyebrows go up and could almost hear her thinking, "My *stepdad's ex-wife* is now part of the Easter program?" I knew that she would later tell her friends the story. Things grew increasingly surreal as the Zoom delay meant that each household sang slightly out of sync from each other. Everyone felt relieved when the hymn ended, except for me, since I now had to play the piano.

I felt nervous about the larger audience, and everyone sang faster than I could play, so I ended up just playing the right-hand notes, which I've heard people call the "treble clef." Inwardly, I felt like this entire plan had reached disaster status. But it got worse! After I finished attempting to accompany our congregational hymn, Jeff asked if any of the grandkids wanted to sing a Primary song. Our daughter-in-law, Gabi, said that they didn't want to sing but that our granddaughter, Markie, wanted to do a dance while Scout played the melodica. As Scout eagerly jumped up to accompany Markie's interpretive dance with a made-up tune, I realized that our Easter program seemed more like a talent show than a worship service.

Partway through our disjointed meeting, I remembered the homemade stained-glass window. I had completely forgotten to pull up the blackout shade to reveal the surprise. I stood up abruptly and raised the shade. The colored tissue paper completely covered the window, and the sun hit it perfectly to make it glow. But no one reacted to it at all. I had expected they would smile or even gasp in delight, but instead, the additional light just made it harder for everyone to see the people on the projector screen. Even though I knew my timing made it more difficult for them to appreciate this unexpected Easter gift, their disinterest took the wind out of my sails.

Our meeting hadn't provided an uplifting spiritual experience, and it had lasted much longer than anyone anticipated. Tay's family had to leave for his in-laws' Easter party, and they no longer had time to eat Egg-la-Daisies with us. Our Zoom breakfast dropped from four households to three. Allie and LJ hadn't read the text about church very closely and thought the Zoom start time represented when we would eat together. So, they had patiently sat through painful musical numbers with cold toast and coagulated white sauce for forty minutes. We hurried to get everyone fed, and although we created lovely little flowers with egg white petals and yolk centers, I felt horrible that our long church meeting had robbed Jeff of the breakfast with all his kids and grandkids that he had planned so carefully.

Our afternoon had a few positive moments, but by the time the kids went back to their dad's house, I felt emotionally exhausted and knew the day had left Jeff completely drained. I offered to pick up the scooters and roller skates that the kids had left in the front yard and headed out by myself so we could both decompress. As I collected toys, I noticed our neighbors heading out for an evening walk with their four smiling children. They all looked so cute and happy, so I called over to them to ask if they wanted me to take their picture since it was Easter Sunday. I knew they had spent the entire day at home, like most people, and probably hadn't gotten a photo of everyone together. They thanked me and quickly sat down on the rocks in front of their house. All the kids cooperated, looked right at the camera, and smiled. No one complained about the delay or argued about where to sit. I took their picture, and they said goodbye. They looked perfect, both in the photo and as they walked down the street, hand in hand.

As I turned and walked back toward my house, I slipped into a downward spiral of self-pity. I felt like our family was in a million pieces. I didn't want to share my kids on holidays or watch Jeff miss his own kids. Our home church had been unnecessarily hectic and stressful. Everything seemed harder than Jeff and I pictured, and we couldn't seem to simplify with everyone's competing agendas and different priorities. I knew I shouldn't compare our blended family to the family across the street, but I indulged those petty feelings as I reviewed our fragmented day. Other families appeared neat, tidy, and cohesive. In contrast, I felt like our family was all over the place, literally and figuratively.

I slowly walked across the asphalt and into our driveway as the last of the evening sun shone on our brick house. Just then, I saw the empty tomb made of tissue paper, and the Holy Ghost pulled up the blackout shade in my mind, allowing a message from God to shine through. The thought came suddenly and clearly: "Your family is like your homemade stained-glass window." I stopped walking and stood completely still so I could focus on the ideas that came into my mind. Through the Spirit, I felt my Heavenly Parents drawing parallels, helping me see how my art project and our blended family were both made up of many separate pieces, coming together at different angles. As I looked at the variety of colors and shapes on the window, I realized that while not a single, unified whole, the juxtaposition of the pieces created something beautiful and conveyed a powerful message. The Holy Ghost testified to my heart that our family, even while lacking tidiness and cohesion, had great value and purpose.

That's when it dawned on me that I had been *prompted* to make the stained-glass window! The Holy Ghost had planted the idea in my mind, but not for my kids. I unknowingly followed a prompting that came because I needed something positive to do on Easter to show my gratitude for the Atonement and Resurrection of Jesus Christ. It fed my soul to have a project and make something even slightly artistic that reflected my testimony. Then, at the end of a long day, it provided the perfect analogy to heal my heavy heart.

I knew that the comforting thought hadn't originated in my discouraged and weary mind. Negative thinking and unfair comparisons do not yield epiphanies. Because that moment became a luminous stone for me, I didn't want it to fade. I didn't want to risk Satan throwing any distractions my way that could disrupt the delicate spiritual memory. So, before I even walked into my house, I took out my phone and dictated a journal entry with a voice recognition app so that I could preserve my exact feelings and thoughts in that quiet moment.

President Eyring has cautioned that we can lose subtle messages from the Holy Ghost within minutes. He said:

> Write down the messages you receive from God. I have found that thc spiritual impression that was clear one minute can be blurred or gone a few minutes later. Even in the middle of the night, I have learned to get up and write down impressions. Otherwise they may be lost.[103]

Thankfully, the act of writing down our stories strengthens them in our minds. And as we send a sign to God that we treasure divine communication, we increase our capacity to receive more revelation. But we acquire another ability at the same time. The act of recording spiritual experiences also demonstrates to Satan that we value and know how to handle sacred things. In this way, each time we successfully receive a message through the Holy Ghost and write about it, our power to withstand Satan increases.

---

103. Henry B. Eyring, "The First Vision: A Pattern for Personal Revelation" *Ensign*, February 2020.

* * *

One effective way to watch the covenant path for luminous stones involves seeking heavenly help. President Eyring counseled us to cast our minds over the previous day and ponder the past-tense questions, "Did God send a message that was just for me?" and, "Did I see His hand in my life or the lives of my children?"[104] We can take that same approach before a new day begins and ask our Father to enable us to recognize revelation as it comes. Elder David A. Bednar taught:

> Meaningful morning prayer is an important element in the spiritual creation of each day—and precedes the temporal creation or actual execution of the day.
>
> Morning and evening prayers—and all of the prayers in between—are not unrelated, discrete events; rather, they are linked together each day and across days, weeks, months, and even years. . . . Such meaningful prayers are instrumental in obtaining the highest blessings God holds in store for His faithful children.[105]

Two years after I made my stained-glass window, I learned more about the power of meaningful morning prayer. At the beginning of Easter weekend in 2022, Kate met a fellow high school student named Isaac Nutall at a public library. They planned to work on student-written legislation for the upcoming debate season. Since they attended schools in different cities, Isaac and Kate had only interacted at tournaments and by text before that afternoon. Sitting at a quiet table in the almost empty library, they discussed their liberal political views and brainstormed potential topics for legislation. Relishing their shared passion for congressional debate, they talked about a wide variety of social issues and the time went quickly. When the librarians started turning off lights and glancing

---

104. Eyring, "O Remember, Remember" *Ensign*, November 2007.
105. David A. Bednar, "Pray Always" *Ensign*, November 2008.

their way, Kate and Isaac packed up their backpacks and started to walk toward the exit.

Just then, a woman rushed up to them and frantically asked, "Do either of you have a laptop I could use? I need to log in to a website and clock the hours I worked this week by five o' clock. And I can't get the website to work on my phone!"

Isaac responded immediately, "Yes, you can use mine!" and quickly handed her his laptop.

After she successfully submitted the online form to her employer, she gratefully told the teenagers, "You guys are the answer to my prayer!"

To her surprise, Isaac replied, "*You* are the answer to *my* prayer!" He then shared with them how every morning, he prays and asks God for an opportunity to serve someone that day.

At that, the woman started to whoop and holler, singing praises in the parking lot. She exclaimed, "The Lord is *good*! You are doing the Lord's work right here!" Stretching her arms up to the sky in a whole-body celebration, she swayed as she continued, "God is with me, God is with you, God is here with us!" Then, she turned to them and pointed out, "It's Good Friday!"

Her contagious enthusiasm still reflected in Kate's eyes when she arrived home twenty minutes later. She radiated as she told the story, laughing as she described how happy the three of them were, Isaac, Kate, and this faith-filled, dancing lady who recognized God's hand and then gave thanks in a county library parking lot. Kate still had pure excitement flowing through her veins from the experience. Isaac also drove home with a happy heart, thankful that the morning prayer he used to spiritually create his day guided him to the woman with the time-card crisis.

He didn't know it and Kate didn't know it, but Isaac also answered my prayers that day. Kate had told me several weeks earlier that she no longer had any friends who shared both her political views and her religious beliefs. She grimly reported that those who once fit into both categories had left the Church. Though she had amazing people in her life that fit one description or the other, I prayed fervently that she could find someone to stand with her in the sparsely populated center of her Venn diagram. Because Isaac watched the path for promptings, he unknowingly revealed specific characteristics that don't often coincide in the teenagers in our area. When I heard about what happened at the library, like the woman in the parking lot who immediately confessed God's hand in all things, I marveled at His goodness.

* * *

When Jesus Christ directed the Nephites to bring forth the record they had kept, He asked if saints appeared and ministered unto many, as Samuel the Lamanite prophesied they would. Similarly, He might ask me if Isaac Nutall appeared in a library, if Ruth appeared at a book club, and if Marshall McDonald appeared at a funeral. I want to make sure my kids know that a temple worker who spoke Japanese appeared in Yuki's sealing room. Elder Rasband appeared at Jeff's early-morning priesthood meeting. And Ron Radcliffe appeared with a new tie for our stake president.

When you "cast [your] mind over the day,"[106] looking for God's influence, the Holy Ghost will help you remember your red rock hoodoos, picnic-style dining room table, ChapStick, manta ray, and countless other conduits of God's love. Can you remember a time when you caught a glimpse of God's love for you? I bet you have time to write one or two sentences about it right now:

____

____

____

____

____

____

106. Henry B. Eyring, "O Remember, Remember" *Ensign*, November 2007.

____

____

____

____

____

____

____

____

Our Heavenly Parents and Jesus Christ have blessed us and our loved ones with tender mercies, ideas, images, feelings, words, and moments that connect us to Them. When we stand still and behold them with spiritual eyes and hear them with spiritual ears, our testimonies will grow into redwood trees. The Savior and His prophets have commanded us to write down the miracles we experience, whether enormous, medium, or breathtakingly microscopic. And as we do, we stand as witnesses with all the record keepers, "for, for this intent have we written these things, that they may know that we knew of Christ."[107]

I testify that luminous stones lie all along the covenant path. Some show up so suddenly, we almost trip over them; others, we must molten ourselves with great effort before Jesus Christ can infuse them with light. May you find peace and power as you watch for luminous stones, save them, and share them with others. I pray that the miracles in your life won't fit in your pockets, and you will joyfully haul them across the riverbed on your shoulders[108] and carry them up the mountain in your hands.[109]

107. Jacob 4:4.
108. Joshua 4:5.
109. Ether 3:1.

ABOUT THE AUTHOR

Rachel Matthews earned a Bachelor's degree in Professional and Technical Writing from Utah State University. In 2013, she started True Story, a business focused on creating and improving nonfiction content. Rachel has a passion for preserving personal stories and transforming family histories into engaging, cohesive narratives that will connect generations. Balancing kids, step kids, and grandkids of all different ages, Rachel understands that it's impossible to remember our subtle, sacred moments unless we document them. Rachel lives with her husband and kids in Utah, where she serves on the Holladay Interfaith Council. She loves attending outdoor community festivals to taste food from other cultures and dance to live music.

Scan the QR code to visit her
website at www.truestorywriting.com